T0332006

The First Amendment in the Trump Era

The First Amendment
in the Trump Era

TIMOTHY ZICK

OXFORD
UNIVERSITY PRESS

The First Amendment in the Trump Era. Timothy Zick.
© Timothy Zick 2019. Published 2019 by Oxford University Press.

OXFORD
UNIVERSITY PRESS

Oxford University Press is a department of the University of Oxford. It furthers the University's
objective of excellence in research, scholarship, and education by publishing worldwide. Oxford is
a registered trademark of Oxford University Press in the UK and certain other countries.

Published in the United States of America by Oxford University Press
198 Madison Avenue, New York, NY 10016, United States of America.

Library of Congress Cataloging-in-Publication Data
Names: Zick, Timothy, author.
Title: The First amendment in the Trump era / Timothy Zick.
Description: New York : Oxford University Press, 2019. | Includes bibliographical references
and index.
Identifiers: LCCN 2019010939 | ISBN 9780190073992 ((hardback) : alk. paper)
Subjects: LCSH: Freedom of expression—United States. | United States—
Politics and government—2017–
Classification: LCC KF4770 .Z53 2019 | DDC 342.7308/53—dc23
LC record available at https://lccn.loc.gov/2019010939

1 3 5 7 9 8 6 4 2

Printed by Integrated Books International, United States of America

Note to Readers
This publication is designed to provide accurate and authoritative information in regard to
the subject matter covered. It is based upon sources believed to be accurate and reliable and
is intended to be current as of the time it was written. It is sold with the understanding that
the publisher is not engaged in rendering legal, accounting, or other professional services.
If legal advice or other expert assistance is required, the services of a competent professional
person should be sought. Also, to confirm that the information has not been affected or
changed by recent developments, traditional legal research techniques should be used,
including checking primary sources where appropriate.

*(Based on the Declaration of Principles jointly adopted by a Committee of the
American Bar Association and a Committee of Publishers and Associations.)*

You may order this or any other Oxford University Press publication
by visiting the Oxford University Press website at www.oup.com.

For all the noisy dissenters—past, present, and future.

Contents

Acknowledgments

This book has been a very unusual project for me. It is less "academic" in nature than my prior works, which I hope will translate into both a wider audience and a broader discourse about its subject matter. The book has presented the usual challenges authors face when they write about important current events—in many instances as they occur. In that sense, the book is a product of the high speed news cycle it sometimes critiques.

In part owing to these challenges, this manuscript has not been widely vetted or presented at various academic conferences. I would, however, like to thank my anonymous reviewers, who each gave me so much to think about in terms of the tone, subject matter, and purpose of the book. In addition to their input, the project benefitted from many conversations with colleagues and friends, some of whom have expertise in free speech and press matters and some who merely have an abiding interest in these topics. I thank them all, as a group, for listening to my concerns and for sharing their own impressions of the Trump Era as it relates to the First Amendment.

I also want to thank, again as a group, the many journalists and reporters who have doggedly pursued the First Amendment concerns that make up the heart of the book. It has been no small task to keep up with the current president's broadsides against First Amendment norms, values, and rights. The media's work in this area, as in many others, demonstrates the necessity of having a free and independent press.

I want to thank the William & Mary Law School for financial support and encouragement.

Last but not least, I want to thank my research assistant, Chantaya Costa, for carefully reviewing the manuscript. Any errors that remain are, of course, my own.

Introduction

An important part of the legacy of the presidency of Donald Trump will be its impact on the First Amendment's free press and speech traditions. The conditions of the "Trump Era," as the book refers to our present moment, pose many challenges for free press and speech. The era, which has been significantly influenced by the many pronouncements of the current president on press and speech concerns, has challenged core First Amendment principles and values. These include the necessity of preserving a free and independent press, the need to protect robust and sometimes caustic criticism of public officials, and the importance of protest and dissent to effective self-government. Although some of candidate and President Trump's actions and proposals have also implicated individual free speech and press rights, the book focuses more broadly on these general principles and values. That said, the general and specific are related; the erosion of the First Amendment's foundations may well lead to the loss of personal free press and speech freedoms. Among many other matters, whether this too will be part of the Trump Era's legacy remains an open question.

The Trump Era

The Trump Era is not the first period in which core First Amendment principles and values have been challenged. The current president is not the first to defy press and speech norms, traditions, and rights. Nor will he likely be the last president to do so. However, the current era has engendered unique First Amendment concerns.

In whatever manner history ultimately classifies the Trump presidency, one of its most exceptional attributes is the open and often contemptuous nature of the president's relationships with the press and with individual dissenters. The difficulties and dysfunctions of those relationships have been on full display in real time. President Trump has used social media to threaten, troll, and retaliate against reporters, media entities, and dissenters. We ought to heed carefully the First Amendment lessons of this era—both to assess any damage done to our free press and speech institutions and traditions, and perhaps as importantly to reacquaint ourselves with the foundations upon which those things rest.

As noted, the "Trump Era," as the book refers to it, is in significant part a product of its namesake. However, the First Amendment challenges we face as a nation are broader and deeper than any single government official. The Trump Era can also be described with reference to a number of characteristics or attributes that predated President Trump and will likely outlast him. These include the precipitous decline of the institutional press, mass digitization of communication, generational uncertainty about the benefits of freedom of speech, deepening social and cultural cleavages along racial and other lines, intense and negative partisanship, the rise of a "post-truth" culture, and the proliferation of hateful expression. President Trump did not cause these things to occur. However, he has taken advantage of these conditions and often exacerbated their negative effects.

One purpose of the book is to catalogue the extraordinary number of instances in which the statements, actions, and reactions of Donald Trump, first as a candidate and then as president of the United States, have questioned or threatened First Amendment values and rights. Some of these events have received abundant news coverage. But others have received only fleeting attention. During the Trump Era, news coverage has jumped from one incendiary statement or action to the next. Owing to the multitude of events that occur in any given "news cycle"—if that is still the right phrase—it is easy to miss the First Amendment forest for the tress.

The book does not merely describe the president's interactions with press and speech freedoms. Rather, it examines their potential implications. To place current First Amendment concerns in appropriate context, the book looks to and applies the lessons of American history.

When it comes to the current era, there is a tendency to suppose that we have been here before. Thus, commentators will often begin their remarks about the First Amendment and other matters by noting that Donald Trump is "not the first president to _____." As we will see, there are indeed historical analogs for many of the president's statements, actions, and policies relating to free press and speech. However, there are also things that are distinctive and unique about both this president and the current era.

For example, unlike his predecessors, President Trump openly boasts to the public about undermining the press and publicly announces, often via social media, retaliatory actions he has taken or intends to take to silence his critics. The book seeks to distinguish the historically analogous from the ahistorical. Some of the differences relate to the uniqueness of the president himself, others to the conditions of the current era, and still others to both.

Challenges to Free Press and Speech

The Trump presidency has cast a spotlight on a number of critically important First Amendment concerns. Significant concerns were first foreshadowed during the 2016 presidential election. Candidate Trump encouraged crowds at his campaign rallies to "rough up" protesters.[1] To deal with terrorist speech, he talked of "shutting down parts of the internet." Candidate Trump called the nation's libel laws a "sham" and vowed to "open up our libel laws, so when [newspapers] write purposely negative and horrible and false articles, we can sue them and win lots of money."[2]

As many commentators and officials have observed, it is not always clear when or whether to take Donald Trump literally or seriously when he makes such statements. However, even assuming that proposals to assault protesters, censor internet speech, and "open up" laws that limit liability for the publication of criticism of public officials are not to be taken literally, the sentiments behind them are deeply troubling and deserve to be taken seriously.

Since Trump was elected president, the nature and scope of the Trump Era's First Amendment challenges have become clearer. President Trump has waged a public and vicious "war" on the media and the press. On several occasions, he and his advisors have called the institutional press "the enemy of the American people" and the "opposition party." The president has called individual reporters or networks "unpatriotic," "crazy," "corrupt," "phony," "dishonest," "failing," "a dope," and "losers."

This "war" is not merely rhetorical. For example, Trump officials have denied White House reporters access to press briefings and other official events, owing to the reporters' "disrespectful" questions or negative coverage. President Trump has threatened to use the powers of his office and of other government departments to punish the media. He has suggested that broadcast licenses be reviewed—and perhaps revoked—in response to negative media coverage. He has encouraged the Senate Intelligence Committee to investigate negative news stories about the Trump administration. The president has also suggested that Congress "look into" the federal tax situation of Amazon, a company owned by Jeff Bezos, who also happens to own a critical news outlet—the *Washington Post* (which the president has referred to as the "Amazon Washington Post"). President Trump has urged the U.S. postmaster general to double the delivery rates charged to Amazon. He has reportedly met with the postmaster to encourage or order that specific course of action.

As president, Trump has frequently vowed to "take a look at the libel laws"—for the clear purpose of making it easier for him to sue critics of his official conduct. The president has also been sharply critical of the press's use of anonymous sources, in some cases even threatening to expose and prosecute them—even in contexts that do not implicate national security.

As part of his self-described "war on the press," President Trump has redefined, popularized, and weaponized the phrase "fake news." He has used the phrase, which actually refers to *intentionally* manufactured content, to refer to any negative coverage of himself or the Trump administration.

President Trump has not been shy about his intentions. He told one interviewer that his attacks on the institutional press are intentional and strategic. They are designed, he said, to undermine the press's credibility and to turn the public against the media.[3] There is evidence that this strategy is working. Public approval of the press is now at historic lows. A recent poll found that more than 40 percent of self-identified Republicans would give the president the power to shut down certain media outlets "engaged in bad behavior."[4] More than 70 percent of respondents agreed that it should be easier to sue reporters when they knowingly publish false information. Perhaps most chilling, a recent Gallup poll indicates that 49 percent of Republicans now view the institutional press as "the enemy of the American people."

All presidents dislike negative press coverage. Some, like Trump, have complained bitterly that the press is "unfair." Some have gone further and taken steps to silence reporters and critics. However, we must be careful with "not the first president to" observations. In both tone and substance, the Trump administration has waged a different sort of "war" on the press and has a different relationship with the First Amendment more generally than other administrations of the modern era. The public labeling of the press as "the enemy of the American people," the transparent and intentional effort to undermine the credibility of the press, and the threats to use the power of the presidency to punish or deter critical reporting are all unique attributes of this presidency. Moreover, the press that went to "war" with prior presidents was much stronger than the fragile and weakened institutional press we have today.

For obvious reasons, journalists and reporters have focused significant attention on the attacks leveled against the institutional press.[5] However, there are many other aspects to what amounts to a much broader "war on dissent." To fully appreciate and understand the First Amendment challenges of the current era, we need to take account of all fronts in this war.

As president, Trump has demonstrated a disturbing inclination to punish his critics. His vow to "open up" the libel laws is just one indication of this general attitude. President Trump has also posted tweets and made public statements suggesting that certain criticisms of himself and the administration are "seditious" and worthy of punishment. He has taken concrete steps to censor or suppress individual critics. For example, President Trump revoked the security clearance of John Brennan, a former CIA director, who has been publicly critical of the president and the Trump administration's national security policies. He has threatened to do the same with respect to other former government officials who have criticized him personally or questioned the administration's policies.

President Trump has insisted on "loyalty"—not only or especially to the government or nation, but also to himself. Reports suggest that he has insisted that some top advisors in the administration sign nondisclosure agreements. Such agreements are common in the private sector. However, they are unprecedented in federal government. The agreements reportedly prohibit officials from disparaging the president, his businesses, or others working in the administration. This goes well beyond restrictions on the sharing of classified and secret information—conduct that is covered by federal laws and regulations. The agreements are another means of suppressing criticism—in this case even by government officials who have separated from federal service.

Other presidential responses to dissent similarly indicate a penchant for equating any criticism with "disloyalty," "treason," or "sedition." For instance, when an anonymous senior official working for the Trump administration published a critical op-ed in the *New York Times*, President Trump suggested that the *Times* identify and "hand over" the person owing to "national security" concerns. The president has also suggested "looking into" Google's algorithm, which he alleges (without any evidence) returns search results that are predominantly "bad" for him and the Trump administration. The apparent implication of such an investigation is that the government would order a private company to include more "positive" search results that reflect favorably on the president or his administration—an action that would violate the First Amendment right against compelled speech. In a demonstration of just how sensitive the current president is to public criticism, he has even suggested that the comedy sketch show *Saturday Night Live* should be "investigated" (presumably by some governmental agency) for the "offense" of broadcasting presidential parodies.

Throughout American history, sedition, subversion, and disloyalty have been attacked and even criminalized—particularly in times of war. In 1798, President Adams had many of his critics jailed pursuant to the Sedition Act of 1798, a federal law that criminalized publication of information critical of government institutions and officials. President Wilson advocated and Congress enacted a second Sedition Act in 1918, in an effort to censor critics of U.S. involvement in World War I.

However, the principles of the modern First Amendment do not tolerate or permit such targeted suppression of dissent. Indeed, the Supreme Court has concluded that suppression of speech critical of government and public officials is directly contrary to "the central meaning of the First Amendment."[6]

To be sure, President Trump's tweets, statements, and actions do not purport to resurrect the old crime of "seditious libel." However, they are unmistakable signals that criticism of government will not be tolerated and may indeed result in investigations, regulations, or other negative consequences. Not for the first time in American history, government is falsely equating dissent and disloyalty. And once again—although to an extent not witnessed in recent eras, and during a time of relative peace rather than wartime—government is attacking and threatening its critics.

The First Amendment challenges of the Trump Era extend beyond concerns about institutional press freedoms and censorship of official critics. In a more general sense, public dissent has been attacked and official orthodoxy and conformity have been insisted upon. Thus, President Trump once suggested that individuals who burn the U.S. flag ought to be jailed and lose their U.S. citizenship—sanctions that would plainly violate the First Amendment, which protects flag-burning.

President Trump has also engaged in a very public and vitriolic fight with National Football League (NFL) players who silently kneeled during the playing of the National Anthem to protest what they viewed as police brutality. The president referred to these dissenters as disloyal and unpatriotic.

Indeed, he made it abundantly clear that he thinks all Americans should stand at attention when the National Anthem is performed—preferably with hands over hearts. President Trump encouraged NFL team owners to fire or fine any player who did not stand respectfully during the playing of the anthem. The president openly castigated the NFL for allowing *any* form of protest during the pregame ceremonies. These statements venture beyond expressing personal disapproval and suggest official reprisals. Thus, the president has suggested that the NFL's antitrust exemption ought to be "looked into" in the event such protests continue. Perhaps not surprisingly, shortly after this statement, the NFL announced a change to its protest policy.

The president's penchant for orthodoxy even extends to holiday greetings and references to God in the Pledge of Allegiance. He has assured the public that Americans will say "Merry Christmas" during the holidays—the latest apparent response to the so-called "War on Christmas." And President Trump has also made a point of publicly drawing attention to the language "under God" in the Pledge, suggesting that Americans emphasize it. In these instances, the president has appealed to a version of Christian nationalism. He has assured a political and demographic minority that "real" Americans will express themselves in a way that comports with that particular minority's preferences and views.

These episodes reprise historical conflicts over enforced orthodoxy regarding matters of nationalism, religion, and politics. The president can certainly encourage certain kinds of expression, and he may express his own viewpoints on patriotism and other matters. However, the First Amendment plainly prohibits government from coercing others to express official viewpoints. In *West Virginia State Board of Education v. Barnette* (1943), the Supreme Court invalidated state laws that required public school children to salute the U.S. flag and recite the Pledge of Allegiance. The Court famously concluded: "If there is any fixed star in our constitutional constellation, it is that no official, high or petty, can prescribe what shall be orthodox in politics, nationalism, religion, or other matters of opinion or force citizens to confess by word or act their faith therein."[7] The Court relied on the same core "anti-orthodoxy" principle when it invalidated state and federal laws that imposed criminal penalties on those who "desecrated" the U.S. flag.[8]

Government demands for "loyalty" also implicate this anti-orthodoxy principle. As the Supreme Court has recognized, laws that demand loyalty to the nation or the Constitution as a condition of employment "cast a pall of orthodoxy" over university classrooms and government offices.[9] As noted, President Trump's demands for loyalty sometimes appear to be more personal in nature, relating to himself and his family. However, the effect is the same—the pressure to conform leads to the same "pall of orthodoxy" as do more nationalistic loyalty requirements.

In sum, President Trump has reprised and re-centered national debates over the imposition of official orthodoxy. Under current First Amendment doctrine, the government cannot demand or compel anyone to accept or articulate its views with respect to nationalism, religion, or other matters. This principle prohibits tyrannical majorities—or tyrannical minorities backed by the government—from imposing their views on the political community.

President Trump has also made clear that he disapproves of public protests and demonstrations. He has labeled political protests "embarrassing" and tweeted that they should not be allowed. During the presidential election, Trump ran as "the law and order candidate." Several early episodes during his presidency suggested that his brand of "law and order" would negatively impact public contention. Indeed, one of the first official acts of the Trump Justice Department was to prosecute hundreds of individuals who attended the president's inauguration in order to protest his election. Prosecutors put large groups of protesters on trial under a "conspiracy to riot" theory, which seemingly did not require actual proof of individual lawbreaking. Prior to the trial, investigators sought computer records from websites that protesters had used to coordinate their inaugural demonstrations. The cases were ultimately dismissed but only after prosecutors failed to prove the cases against the first batch of protesters. Federal prosecutors also charged a single protester who attended the confirmation hearing of Attorney General Jefferson Sessions. The woman was arrested for unlawful protest after she chuckled aloud at an answer the nominee gave to a question about civil rights. After a judge threw out the conviction, before ultimately dismissing the charges the Justice Department considered retrying the case.

Reversing a policy adopted by President Obama, the Trump administration ordered that federal funds be made available to state and local police departments. These funds can be directed toward outfitting police with riot gear and other protest policing equipment. In the wake of the Trump inaugural protests and other high-profile demonstrations, several states proposed laws clamping down on public protests. The measures included increased penalties for blocking traffic and provisions absolving careless drivers of liability for colliding with protesters in the streets. These proposals are in line with the president's own "law and order" policies and pronouncements.

The American Revolution was fueled by public displays, including parades, pickets, and demonstrations. Public protests and contention also facilitated the Constitution's founding. Many battles have since been waged to secure access to public properties and other First Amendment protections for demonstrations, protests, and other means of public dissent. Citing the need for public safety and order, governments have long sought to control and manage access to public properties and public protests. Civil libertarians have pushed back by demanding breathing space for speech critical of segregation, limits on women's suffrage, war, and other matters of public concern.

In the past, access battles focused primarily on public streets, parks, and sidewalks. Speakers and assemblies ultimately gained a measure of access to these places. In the digital era, protesters and other speakers have demanded access to modern public forums such as government websites and official social media pages. President Trump's Twitter page has become a symbolic focal point concerning access to public officials in the digital era. The president has made unprecedented use of Twitter and social media, both to communicate his personal views and to announce important government policies. When he blocked a number of critics who posted negative comments in response to his tweets, they sued him for violating their First Amendment rights. A federal district court concluded that the comments section of the President's Twitter account is a "public forum" and ruled that blocking critics violated the First Amendment.[10] The case, which is currently being appealed, will have important implications for citizens' ability to interact and communicate with public officials who use social media.

The Trump Era has also highlighted the lessons of the First Amendment's relationship with hateful and derogatory speech—an aspect of dissent that raises some unique complications. In the United States, government cannot censor or punish speech on the ground that it denigrates or offends individuals based on their race, ethnicity, or other characteristics. Although the sentiments and opinions expressed are deeply offensive and hurtful, the First Amendment generally protects the right to convey them. This approach is exceptional. Other developed democracies outlaw certain kinds of hateful and derogatory speech. Although the law is settled, Americans continue to debate the extent to which the First Amendment *ought* to cover "hate speech."

The Trump presidency and administration have placed the issue of "hate speech" front and center in several respects. The president has himself communicated hateful and derogatory speech about Mexicans, women, the disabled, and others. When he famously said, in response to the alt-right rally in Charlottesville, Virginia, during the summer of 2017, that there were fine people "on both sides," President Trump highlighted the significant harms that "hate speech" can produce. When then-Attorney General Jefferson Sessions publicly criticized university speech policies that punished students for certain forms of hateful and derogatory speech, he failed to mention or acknowledge the harms associated with such communications. Instead, he chided students who sought some relief from harmful "hate speech" and politicized the issue.

Although it has taken a free-speech-protective position consistent with current First Amendment doctrine, the Trump administration has done a very poor job of explaining or defending the First Amendment's protection for "hate speech." The administration has missed obvious and important opportunities to educate citizens and officials with regard to the intersection between freedom of speech and equality, and the relationship between derogatory speech and dissent. Instead, as with so many important issues, it has politicized "hate speech." The president has bemoaned the "politically correct" left, which condemns such expression despite the protection afforded to it under the First Amendment. Seeking to leverage the politics of "hate speech," the president issued an executive order requiring universities to protect free speech and other First Amendment rights on campus—something public universities are already required to do, and private universities generally endeavor to do.

As these examples demonstrate, the First Amendment controversies and challenges of the Trump Era implicate a number of historical lessons concerning freedom of speech and freedom of the press. Those lessons are intertwined with and informed by the principal justifications for the First Amendment's free speech and press provisions. First Amendment free press and speech rights facilitate citizen self-government, encourage the pursuit of knowledge and truth, check governmental abuse, and protect speaker autonomy.[11] During the Trump Era, each of these functions has been challenged, sometimes in uniquely troublesome ways.

As the discussion indicates, the book is highly critical of the president's and the administration's attitudes respecting, and general approach to, the First Amendment. Taken together, the president's public statements and actions indicate a distressing lack of knowledge of, and respect for, First Amendment principles, values, and rights. President Trump's brand of would-be authoritarianism poses an exceptional danger to the First Amendment. However, even if in many instances the president is not to be taken literally, the Trump Era provides an opportunity to consider—or in many cases reconsider—some of our most cherished First Amendment commitments. The lessons highlighted in the chapters that follow are as relevant in the present era as they have ever been—indeed, perhaps even more so.

Ultimately, the book's advocacy is not in favor of or against a particular individual or public official, but rather in defense of the First Amendment's free press and speech protections. It invites readers to reflect upon the manner in which the Trump administration has performed as a steward of our First Amendment traditions and institutions. We have reached a critical moment in our nation's history and politics, one in which public regard for core First Amendment values, institutions, and rights appears to be dissipating. This, then, is a most appropriate time to consider how we can best defend and preserve our First Amendment.

The President as Speaker and Subject

Although the book generally seeks to avoid constitutional jargon and legal technicalities as much as possible, a couple of issues need to be dealt with up front. The first relates to the distinction between government's function as a regulator of private speech and its role as a speaker or communicator. The other pertains to the question of whether the First Amendment's free press and speech provisions constrain the president.

Governments and public officials can act both as regulators of speech and as speakers. When the government regulates the speech of its citizens, the First Amendment applies with full force to its actions. One central requirement is that government must remain neutral with regard to the content of the private speech it regulates. However, the First Amendment's "government speech" doctrine recognizes that when governments and public officials act as speakers rather than as regulators of private expression, they are not bound by the First Amendment's content-neutrality rule.[12]

The reasons for this content-neutrality exception are complex but trace back to principles of representative government. The Supreme Court has reasoned that if voters are displeased with what the government is communicating with regard to its policies and agendas, they can change representatives at the next election. So, when President Trump communicates his views about libel law, or the NFL, or trade agreements, or his "America First" policies, he is typically engaged in a form of "government speech" or perhaps a form of private speech (depending on the specific context). When he communicates in either of these capacities, the president need not remain neutral.

By contrast, when the president uses the powers of his office to suppress criticism or regulate the speech of others, the First Amendment applies with full force. As a regulator, the president cannot suppress or punish speech because he disagrees with the message or viewpoint communicated or because it is critical of him or the Trump administration. As officials and citizens, presidents are entitled to express their opinions. However, when what they say has or leads to regulatory effects, the First Amendment applies. This distinction between communicating and regulating is relevant to a number of the issues discussed in the book.

The second, and related, issue concerns the legal ramifications of presidential actions that qualify as regulations of private press or speech activities. A few scholars have argued that the president is not formally bound by the words of the First Amendment, and thus cannot be held liable for violating its terms. The text begins, "*Congress* shall make no law . . ." A literal reading of these words suggests that only Congress can be held liable for violating free speech, press, and other First Amendment rights.[13]

The textual and historical arguments supporting this narrow construction are interesting and not without some merit. However, the Supreme Court has never interpreted the First Amendment as applying solely to the legislative branch of government. Further, most scholars have interpreted the First Amendment as restraining *all three* branches of the federal government. In line with this majority view, the book assumes that the First Amendment applies to, and sometimes limits, the president's actions.

While these two issues are important to litigants and scholars, they are not central to the First Amendment lessons examined in the book. In general, those lessons do not focus on whether the president is acting as a regulator or speaker. Nor do they turn on whether he has violated individuals' First Amendment rights, or whether a speaker, reporter, or other individual can sue him in his official capacity for such violations. Rather, the focus of the book will be on the extent to which the Trump Era has been characterized by an erosion of the values, principles, and purposes of freedom of speech and freedom of press.

Chapter Summaries

In terms of organization, the book focuses on six separate but related First Amendment concerns raised during the Trump Era. As the chapters show, these concerns did not originate during the current era. However, the unique conditions of the Trump Era have highlighted and exacerbated them.

Chapter 1 discusses the fragility and necessity of a free and independent press. After detailing the current administration's historically exceptional "war" on the media, the chapter places the Press Clause of the First Amendment in historical and constitutional perspective and discusses the many challenges facing the modern institutional press. The chapter considers both the core functions and the inevitable excesses of a truly free and independent press. It argues that if democracy itself is to survive, a free and independent press must be protected and preserved despite its excesses. Although his publicly declared "war on the press" is unique, President Trump is hardly the first chief executive to attack and challenge the press. Although there are serious questions about the proper scope of First Amendment protection for falsehoods and defamatory statements—including as they relate to public officials—the president's principal goal in raising these concerns is to suppress critical news coverage. Current interpretations of the Press Clause, combined with the potential collapse of laws and norms protecting a free and independent press, pose a critical stress test for the institution's survival. As recent events around the world have shown, we ought not to take the existence of a free and independent press for granted.

Chapter 2 examines the concept of "sedition" and its relation to effective public dissent. President John Adams used the Sedition Act of 1798 to prosecute and jail his critics and political opponents. This episode ultimately led the Supreme Court to conclude that the "central meaning of the First Amendment" is that Americans must be free to criticize their public officials—even if that criticism is caustic and unpleasant. That lesson has been hard-learned, as governments have long sought to suppress "seditious" expression. The current government is no exception to this pattern—although its pursuit of critics is exceptional, in part, in the sense that sedition has historically been targeted mainly during wartime. Although federal and state officials have not proposed reviving the crime of seditious libel, critics of the Trump administration have come under sustained fire and some have suffered tangible consequences for criticizing the president and the administration. The authoritarian urge to punish official critics is a natural byproduct of expansive executive power, and the current president has aggressively pushed the boundaries of executive independence. Punishing or retaliating against critics of official conduct ignores the "central meaning" and central lessons of the First Amendment. It chills expression on matters of public concern, diminishes the prospects for self-government, and stifles dissent.

Chapter 3 examines the "anti-orthodoxy principle," which holds that governments cannot compel or prescribe what thoughts or gestures are acceptable in the realms of politics, culture, or faith. President Trump's public dispute with NFL players and owners over pregame protests, his proposal to criminalize flag-burning and denaturalize flag burners, and his insistence on loyalty all implicate the anti-orthodoxy principle. The First Amendment does not allow government to compel convention and conformity. Its anti-orthodoxy principle is rooted in respect for speaker autonomy and freedom to dissent. The president's statements and actions have challenged Americans to once again tolerate and even embrace peaceful forms of dissent and the communication of diverse views regarding patriotism, social justice, and race.

Chapter 4 examines the First Amendment's lessons relating to the preservation of access to public properties for the purpose of facilitating speech and assembly. Speakers and groups have fought long and hard to obtain and preserve First Amendment rights to use what are referred to as "public forums"—places that the government owns or controls, but that are held in trust for the people for the purpose of exercising First Amendment rights. The "law and order" agenda of the Trump Era, coupled with the president's open disdain for political protest, has revived concerns about ensuring adequate breathing space for public dissent. There are troubling signs that Trump Era "law and order" policies will again lead to sharp limits on the exercise of First Amendment rights. In addition, President Trump's efforts to block critics from his Twitter page foreshadow the next great battle over public space, as dissenters seek access to what the Supreme Court has called "the modern public square." Allowing presidents and other officials to block critics in these spaces raises serious concerns about access to public officials and representatives in the digital age.

Chapter 5 discusses Trump Era controversies relating to "hate speech." The president has been both a purveyor and defender of hateful and derogatory expression. The chapter provides a brief primer on First Amendment protection for "hate speech." It then examines both the harms associated with "hate speech" and the principal justifications for protecting it. The Trump administration has taken a strong stand in favor of preserving the First Amendment status quo as it relates to this kind of content. However, instead of acknowledging the complexities involved, including the harms that "hate speech" inflicts, the administration has generally relied on lazy tropes relating to "political correctness" and has sought to politicize the issue. It has added insult to the injury of "hate speech" by minimizing its harms and failing to educate the public about why such speech ought to be tolerated. In general, this approach has negatively affected political discourse, including on college campuses—where many recent flare-ups have focused on the communication of hateful views and ideas. The chapter examines why "hate speech" is mostly protected speech. It also addresses the extent to which the Trump administration—and other governments—can use their voices to educate Americans about the need to preserve *both* freedom of speech and the security and equal dignity that "hate speech" undermines.

Chapter 6 addresses a concept that connects all of the subjects discussed in previous chapters: dissent. Dissent is itself a central First Amendment concern. As the chapters show, the Trump Era has been characterized by efforts to restrict or suppress dissent in a variety of ways. The chapter begins with a brief discussion of the meaning of dissent. It then turns to the various democratic and social values associated with the communication of dissent. The American Revolution demonstrated that dissent is the lifeblood of democracy. Since that time, however, Americans have not consistently supported or even always tolerated dissent. Cultivating and preserving a culture of dissent is critically important to American democracy. However, during the Trump Era, disrespect for dissent has emanated from the top levels of government. But this is not solely an official problem. Anti-dissent attitudes are far too prevalent in the American political community at large. Despite many obstacles and limits, dissenters have always managed to help defeat authoritarian impulses. Whether a politically polarized, digitally siloed, institutionally challenged, and incessantly distracted political community can effectively resist the current authoritarian forces is a—perhaps *the*—central concern of the Trump Era. The chapter concludes with a discussion of some steps that can be taken to nurture a culture of dissent.

1

A Free and Independent Press

We are aware that the press has, on occasion, grossly abused the freedom it is given by the Constitution. All must deplore such excesses. In an ideal world, the responsibility of the press would match the freedom and public trust given it. But from the earliest days of our history, this free society, dependent as it is for its survival upon a vigorous free press, has tolerated some abuse.[1]

One of the most important First Amendment lessons of the Trump Era relates to the fragility and necessity of a free and independent press. For a number of reasons, the Trump Era is a uniquely precarious time for the institutional press. Even before Trump's election, press independence and freedom rested on far shakier constitutional and legal foundations than most Americans—including many journalists—likely realized. The president's self-proclaimed "war" on the institutional press, which has included his frequent charge that the press is "the enemy of the American people," has threatened to do lasting damage to press freedoms. Evidence suggests that the president may be winning his "war." A recent Gallup poll indicates that nearly half of Republicans now view the press as "the enemy of the American people."

Long before Donald Trump became a candidate for the presidency, digitization of content, diminished revenues, unfavorable market conditions, loss of public support, and other forces were already plaguing the institutional press. Trump has accelerated and exacerbated the media's various challenges. As a candidate and as president, Trump has waged a constant, public, and vitriolic war against the press.[2] He has hurled insults at individual reporters and journalists, referring to them as "fake," "horrible," and "disgusting." As mentioned, President Trump has frequently referred to the institutional press (or some of them, at least) as "the enemy of the American people." He has suggested jailing, punishing, or otherwise retaliating against

The First Amendment in the Trump Era. Timothy Zick.
© Timothy Zick 2019. Published 2019 by Oxford University Press.

specific reporters and media outlets. The White House has denied some reporters access to official events based on the critical nature of their reporting. The president has threatened to use (indeed may have already used) the power of his office to punish or retaliate against media owners and outlets, through such means as higher postal rates and antitrust policies. He has repeatedly vowed to change, or look into changing, the rules governing defamation of public officials like himself—with the intention of making it easier for officials like presidents to sue their press and other critics. Finally, as this book is going to press, the Trump administration indicted Julian Assange, the WikiLeaks founder, under the Espionage Act for publishing diplomatic cables and other secret information. This action may have significant implications for the institutional press, which likewise publishes leaked confidential and secret information.

Along with the many factors already affecting the functioning of the press, relentless attacks by a uniquely vocal and media-constant president have generated serious concerns about the future of the institutional press. As two free press scholars recently observed, "Contrary to widespread belief, our concern should not be that Trump might be taking the first step toward crippling the power of the free press, but rather that he might be taking the final step in a process that has long been underway."[3]

We live in a globally uncertain time for press freedoms. In the past few years, record numbers of reporters have been killed—many outside war zones, where this danger has always been present. In nations across the world—from Poland, to Brazil, to Hungary, to Saudi Arabia—governments have commandeered, restricted, or sought to silence critical press organs and individual reporters. What is happening in the United States, which has long been considered a beacon of press freedom and independence, has worldwide implications. Autocratic leaders, taking their cue from the American president, have railed against the "fake news" and taken steps to censor the press. Meanwhile, in the United States, the war on the press raises critical questions about the viability and health of American democracy itself.

The President's "War" on the Press

As indicated, both as a candidate and through the first term of his presidency, Trump has been a relentless critic of both the institutional press and individual reporters. Of course, presidents have always complained about negative press coverage. A few, including Franklin Roosevelt, John F. Kennedy, and Richard Nixon, have gone further and retaliated or threatened to retaliate against press critics. Americans only found out about these actions long after they were committed. In contrast, the current president takes great pride in publicly attacking and retaliating against the press. He regularly brags about these actions in tweets and at campaign-style rallies. In contrast to President Trump, no former president publicly declared "war" on the press or repeatedly referred to the press as "the enemy of the American people."

In these respects, the character and extent of President Trump's declared "war" on the press are indeed historically unique. Owing to significant concerns about press independence and freedom, PEN America, an association of writers and other literary and media professionals, recently filed a First Amendment lawsuit against President Trump to enjoin his press war.[4] The allegations in the complaint provide a chilling summary of the extent to which the president has thus far sought to undermine press independence and restrict press freedoms.

PEN's legal complaint alleges that President Trump has "violated the First Amendment, and his oath to uphold the Constitution, through directives to administration officials to take retaliatory actions and credible public threats to use his government powers against those who report the news in ways he does not welcome."[5] The complaint notes that from the announcement of his candidacy through his second year in office, the president has sent more than 1,300 critical, insulting, or threatening tweets about the media. Although they may chill reporting and inhibit press freedoms, the president's tweets are not the basis for the lawsuit. Rather, the complaint alleges that the president has taken the following retaliatory *actions*:

- "suspending the White House press credentials of reporters who the President believes failed to show him sufficient 'respect';
- revoking and threatening to revoke security clearances from former government officials who have engaged in public commentary, including on CNN and NBC, because they expressed criticism of the current Administration;
- issuing an executive order to raise postal rates to punish online retailer Amazon.com because Jeff Bezos, its chief shareholder and CEO, owns the *Washington Post*, whose coverage of his Administration the President finds objectionable;

- directing the Department of Justice to challenge a vertical merger between Time Warner and AT&T because of his antagonism to Time Warner subsidary CNN and its news coverage of his Administration; and
- threatening to revoke NBC's and other television stations' broadcast licenses in retaliation for coverage the President dislikes."[6]

The First Amendment allows the president to criticize the press, including on the basis of the content of its coverage. However, as the PEN complaint observes, "Although the President is free to criticize the press, he cannot use the power and authority of the United States government to punish and stifle it."[7]

This is the distinction between government-as-speaker and government-as-regulator discussed in this book's introduction. The distinction cuts to the very core of the First Amendment's protection of a free and independent press. It is patently clear that official retaliation against the press violates the First Amendment. Under Supreme Court precedents, it is also clear that the press and other speakers have wide latitude to publish criticism of the actions of government officials.[8] One critically important question we must face during the Trump Era is whether the core is solid enough to withstand the conditions under which the modern press operates.

Constitutional Foundations of a Free and Independent Press

The media and institutional press face distinctive challenges during the Trump Era. Those challenges are occurring against a backdrop concerning press rights and freedoms that long predates the election of the current president. To better understand the press's current situation, it is first necessary to consider some important background information concerning the nature and extent of the protection afforded to "the press" under the U.S. Constitution.

The examination reveals a far narrower conception of press rights than one encounters in current debates about the First Amendment's protection of the media. In particular, it casts doubt on conventional wisdom that the First Amendment expressly protects the institutional press and grants it broad, special constitutional rights. The reality is that much of what counts as press "freedom" is more a function of official grace than constitutional right. And as the Trump presidency shows, official grace can be narrowed or even eliminated depending on who is in charge of providing it.

In political debate and commentary, Americans are fond of pointing to the Constitution's words to support their views. So let's start with the text of the First Amendment. Defenders of "the press" may take some comfort in the fact that the First Amendment explicitly provides that the government cannot abridge "the freedom of the press."

However, as discussed later in the chapter, the Press Clause has not been interpreted as referring to the corporate media or bestowing any special rights on the institutional press. The Press Clause protects individual rights, and those rights are generally coextensive with the rights enjoyed by members of the public. Indeed, as one commentator has observed, "as a matter of positive law, the Press Clause actually plays a rather minor role in protecting the freedom of the press."[9]

In general, the Press Clause has not been interpreted as the special province of the institutional media or professional journalists. Rather, the Supreme Court has interpreted the Press Clause as granting protection to *the people* to gather, publish, and distribute information.[10] Constitutionally speaking, then, cable news companies, newspapers, bloggers, social media posters, and lonely pamphleteers are all "the press." As one prominent First Amendment scholar has described this interpretation, the "press" is a *technology* and not an *industry*.[11] As we will see, this populist conception of "the press" affords the institutional press some important protections. However, those protections have little to do with the Press Clause itself.

From a Founding Era perspective, the "technology" interpretation makes sense. In the eighteenth century, media organizations and professional journalists did not yet exist. Although the records relating to the adoption of the First Amendment are sparse, the Founders likely viewed the publication and distribution of the *Federalist Papers*, which argued in favor of adoption of the proposed Constitution, as part of the American *free speech and press* tradition.

From the Supreme Court's initial consideration of the Press Clause, its decisions adopted this broader meaning of "press." For example, decisions handed down in the 1930s and 1940s treated the claims of pamphleteers, leafleteers, newspaper publishers, book publishers, and others as raising free speech *and free press* concerns.[12]

The Court likely found this broad interpretation attractive for a number of reasons. The Founders themselves frequently used "freedom of the press" and "freedom of speech" interchangeably, leading some scholars to conclude that the two rights effectively overlapped with one another.[13] Further, interpreting the Press Clause as an individual right belonging to all the people allowed the Court to avoid difficult line-drawing questions regarding who or what qualified as "the press."[14] Singling out a special set of persons or organizations would have placed the government in the position of defining which publishers were considered worthy of protection under the Press Clause. This exercise would have been in tension with the First Amendment's rejection of the practice of press licensure.[15]

To be sure, not everyone agrees with this understanding of freedom of the press. Justice Potter Stewart maintained that the Press Clause protected certain institutional rights that were related to important structural functions. He argued that while the Free Speech Clause protected an individual right of expression, the Press Clause protected the *institutional* rights of a "Fourth Estate."[16] Justice Stewart's interpretation had some support from some prominent early First Amendment scholars.[17] More recently, scholars have advocated an interpretation of the Press Clause that differentiates it from the Free Speech Clause, including in some cases recognition of an institutional component.[18] However, the Supreme Court has not shown any inclination to adopt these institutional interpretations. Indeed, the Court has not shown any particular interest at all in the Press Clause, having decided no major press cases in the last several decades.

Thus, in general, the Press Clause has been treated as interchangeable with the Free Speech Clause.[19] It is "complementary to and a natural extension of Speech Clause liberty."[20] More generally, freedom of the press is part of a system of "freedom of expression" that includes other First Amendment rights—speech, assembly, and petition.[21] In sum, the actual status and scope of the Press Clause is significantly at odds with confident claims that freedom of the press is secure owing to its explicit textual recognition.

First Amendment "Press" Rights

The Supreme Court has not entirely ignored the press. As discussed further later in this chapter, its decisions have frequently touted a number of virtues associated with a free and independent press. However, as noted, the Court has never articulated any distinctive doctrines or rights that apply specifically to the institutional press. In general, the institutional press—professional journalists and the corporate media—have no greater First Amendment rights than those enjoyed by other "speakers" under the Free Speech Clause.[22]

The rights typically associated with the Press Clause include freedom from prior restraints on publication—orders and injunctions prohibiting content from being disseminated, in contrast to the imposition of liability after publication. In fact, early interpretations of speech and press rights were actually limited to this protection. In his famous *Commentaries*, a treatise that was widely influential in early debates about the American Constitution, William Blackstone wrote that freedom of the press was limited to "laying no previous restraints upon publication, and not in freedom from censure for criminal matter when published."[23] Dean Leonard Levy's influential early work on press freedom agreed that the historical record supported this interpretation of the Press Clause.[24] At the beginning of the twentieth century, the Supreme Court expressed support for this narrow interpretation.[25]

Americans accustomed to thinking of press freedoms as far more robust might be shocked that the Founders may have had such a narrow understanding of press rights. Although the records are sparse, we do know that freedom of the press was a central concern of the Founders.[26] The generation that framed and ratified the First Amendment was acutely aware that the American Revolution likely would not have occurred absent a free and independent press. When they drafted the text of the First Amendment, the Founders borrowed heavily from early state charters. All provided for a press freedom—by contrast, only one provided expressly for the freedom of speech.[27]

Moreover, the Founders likely viewed freedom of the press as performing important democratic functions. Professor Akhil Amar, a leading authority on the Bill of Rights, has argued that at the Founding, rights of speech, assembly, press, and petition all served the basic purpose of restraining the powers granted to the new central government.[28] As demonstrated during the American Revolution, rights to communicate, assemble, publish, and petition government had enabled ordinary citizens to resist tyranny and governmental abuse.[29]

Again, these rights belonged not to an institutional or corporate press but to the people. As quickly became clear, however, the people's press freedoms could be severely restricted. For example, as discussed in more detail in Chapter 2, the First Congress, which included many Founders, enacted the Alien and Sedition Acts of 1798. The Sedition Act criminalized publications that were critical of the president and other government institutions, including Congress. Newspaper publishers and others who published criticism of President John Adams were prosecuted and jailed under the Act. Although the Supreme Court never reviewed its constitutionality, lower courts rejected First Amendment and other constitutional challenges to the Sedition Act. President Jefferson later pardoned those convicted under the Act, and Congress ultimately authorized refunds of the fines paid. However, for an extended period of American history, it was not entirely clear that punishment of "seditious" publications violated the First Amendment.

The Sedition Act controversy shows that notwithstanding the existence of the Press Clause and the recognition of the importance of press freedoms to democracy, the Founding generation authorized the jailing of presidential and government critics. Although it is now infamous, this episode shows that the Founders did not have the broad understanding of press rights that modern Americans associate with the Press Clause. It also indicated that the Founders had not fully internalized some of the important democratic lessons of the Revolutionary Era, specifically as they related to the necessity of a free and independent press. Whatever it was, the "press" could hardly serve its important functions if publishers could be jailed for merely criticizing government.

Even after the Sedition Act disappeared, newspapers and other publishers were hardly free to criticize government and government officials. State defamation laws, which imposed civil and in some cases criminal liability for publishing false statements of fact about public officials, were frequently used to punish newspapers and other publishers. These laws generally imposed a form of strict liability: they *presumed* damages to individual reputation from the mere publication of any false assertions. They also placed the burden on the publisher to prove the truth of any and all assertions of fact. When it came to critical reporting concerning public officials, this could prove to be an impossible burden.

Since it was not made applicable to the states until the 1930s, the First Amendment was not an available defense in state defamation lawsuits. This situation did not drastically change until the 1960s, when the Supreme Court held that state defamation laws had to conform to the First Amendment's free speech and press provisions. In *New York Times Co.*

v. Sullivan, the Court held that when they sued for allegedly false statements relating to the conduct of their official duties, government officials could not recover damages unless they proved that the statements were made with "actual malice"—knowledge that they were false or reckless disregard for their truth.[30] Truth could no longer be made a defense in such cases, and the plaintiff bore the burden of proving both falsity and "actual malice." These, incidentally, are the rules that President Trump has repeatedly vowed to reconsider or "open up" on the ground that they under-protect the reputations of public officials like himself.

The Supreme Court's reasons for creating a special liability rule were rooted in principles of self-government and the pursuit of truth. The Court observed that "although the Sedition Act was never tested in this Court, the attack upon its validity has carried the day in the court of history."[31] Historical events, the Court wrote, "reflect a broad consensus that the Act, because of the restraint it imposed upon criticism of government and public officials, was inconsistent with the [First Amendment]." The Court concluded that the nation's experience with the Sedition Act, and with the offense of seditious libel more generally, had "first crystallized a national awareness of *the central meaning of the First Amendment*.[32] That "central meaning" was that Americans must be free, subject to narrow restrictions, to criticize public officials—even if, the Court emphasized, their statements "include vehement, caustic, and sometimes unpleasantly sharp attacks."

The Court acknowledged that false statements of fact could harm official reputations. However, it reasoned that even false statements about public officials may add something of value to public debate—particularly as they clash with true statements addressing the same subject. In any event, the Court reasoned, false statements were an inevitable aspect of public debate that is intended to be, in the Court's famous characterization, "uninhibited, robust, and wide-open."[33] To hold publishers liable for every false statement would cast a "pall of fear and timidity" over critics of public officials and their actions and thus undermine efforts to hold officials accountable to the people.[34]

New York Times Co. v. Sullivan was a monumental decision. The Court seemed to have finally buried the Sedition Act. Further, it had recognized a right to engage in vigorous and critical reporting concerning public officials. However, consistent with its general treatment of the Press Clause, the Court did not limit defamation standards to the institutional media. Instead, it wrote in broad terms of the freedoms of speech *and* press. Like others, the decision did not create a special liability rule applicable only to corporate media entities. The defamation rules apply whether the defendant is a corporate media giant or a lonely pamphleteer.

In addition to First Amendment protections against prior restraints on publication and limits on defamation liability, today the institutional press enjoys a number of other rights—all, however, by virtue of the Free Speech Clause. That provision generally prohibits government from regulating publications based on their content. It also limits liability for invasion of privacy and intentional infliction of emotional distress.[35] Thus far, is has protected the publication of truthful information lawfully obtained by the press. Like any other "speaker," a newspaper or broadcast outlet enjoys these and other basic free speech rights.

Some press scholars have argued that while these general First Amendment protections are important, insofar as the institutional press is concerned they are substantially incomplete. For instance, under current doctrine, the institutional press has no greater access to government property, proceedings, or information than do members of the general public.[36] Thus, Professor Sonja West has argued that the Court should recognize a Press Clause "newsgathering" right.[37] Moreover, in the early 1970s, the Court held that the Press Clause does not protect reporters from government demands for information about confidential sources.[38] Consistent with its prior decisions, in these contexts the Court refused to view the institutional press as constitutionally "special."

Legal and Non-legal Support for Press Freedoms

As explained, the modern foundation for a free and independent press cannot rest on specific or special First Amendment press rights. Rather, as scholars have observed, this foundation rests on "a mishmash of legal and non-legal privileges and protections."[39]

For example, many states have laws that recognize a limited press privilege in response to subpoenas for confidential source information.[40] However, these and other institutional press protections vary widely. Because they are not mandated by the First Amendment, they can be amended or eliminated through the ordinary legislative process.

The non-legal protections for the institutional press include the institutional press's financial strength, judicial support for press freedoms, public attitudes concerning the importance of a free and independent press, and political norms and customs that created a cooperative, mutually beneficial, and respectful relationship between the press and government officials.[41] However, as scholars have observed, in recent years all of these "pillars" have been significantly weakened or eroded.[42]

Newspapers and other media have been hit hard by declining subscriptions and other economic and market forces. The general economic decline has affected newsgathering, both at home and abroad. Lack of resources has affected the nature and character of reporting and news content. In the courts, the downturn has even limited the press's ability to defend against defamation and other claims.

As scholars have observed, judicial support for press rights has also diminished.[43] In prior historical periods, courts regularly touted the importance of a free and independent press to American democracy. They were inclined to defer to media editorial and other determinations. However, there is now substantial evidence that judicial support for, and deference to, the institutional media have declined.

As noted earlier, in recent decades, the Supreme Court has accepted very few "press" cases for review.[44] Meanwhile, in the lower courts, judges are less likely to defer to journalistic judgments in privacy and other press cases. These cases often turn on whether material is considered "newsworthy," a determination that greatly affects whether a publication is protected by the First Amendment.[45] In recent years, data indicate that the institutional media have lost defamation cases at a higher rate, and at higher costs, relative to prior eras. As discussed earlier, the Supreme Court has long collapsed the Press Clause into the Free Speech Clause, declining to recognize any explicit or special press rights. Even the Court's statements about the press, both in terms of issued decisions and by justices at public events, have gone from overwhelmingly positive to far more skeptical.[46]

Public support for the institutional press is now at an all-time low.[47] As free press scholars RonNell Jones and Sonja West have observed, "In the 1970s, more than two-thirds of Americans reported that they had trust and confidence in the mass media."[48] That number has steadily declined ever since. Jones and West observe that "[a]t the beginning of the Trump presidency . . . press confidence dropped to its lowest level in Gallup polling history."[49] Indeed, positive opinions of the institutional press have recently rested at levels below also-historically-low positive opinions concerning the president himself.

As with the other aspects of the non-legal environment, there are many causes for the decline. Some relate to the media's own conduct and coverage, which is subject to serious criticism. Others are the product of a decades-long coordinated campaign—including most recently by President Trump—to undermine public trust in the media. As Jones and West have concluded, "The once-sturdy pillar of public support that has long sustained the freedom of the press is now slight."[50]

Finally, as Jones and West have also observed, the mutual dependence and symbiosis that once characterized the relationship between the institutional press and government officials has also substantially eroded.[51] As President Trump's use of Twitter makes abundantly clear, officials no longer need the press as they once did to communicate their messages. Relatedly, the institutional press, which relied on officials for access to information and events, now has a more precarious claim on access to such things. Today, Americans receive less and less of their information and news from mainstream media outlets. This has further weakened their position.

Constitutionally, legally, and non-legally, the institutional press is a more fragile and uncertain part of our constitutional democracy than many Americans—including members of the institutional press—appreciate. The Press Clause does not grant any special protections to the institutional press. The Free Speech Clause is not a substitute repository for special media rights. The legal and non-legal environment in which the institutional press operates is increasingly hostile to media rights, decisions, and functions. As these trends demonstrate, there is no ironclad guarantee we will always have a free and independent press.

These negative press realities all preceded the Trump presidency and the Trump Era. However, President Trump's persistent assault on media functions and norms has exacerbated concerns about the fragility of the institutional press. During the Trump Era, we are not likely to see marked improvements in the media's constitutional, legal, or non-legal environments. Indeed, things are likely to get worse. One concern is that the Trump Era will be the straw that breaks the institutional press's back. Again, as Professors Jones and West have observed, "Contrary to widespread belief, our concern should not be that Trump might be taking the *first step* toward crippling the power of the free press, but rather that he might be taking the *final step* in a process that has long been underway."[52]

The Necessary but Imperfect Press

American history shows that a free and independent press is necessary to a functioning democracy. However, during the Trump Era there is a danger that this lesson will be lost to partisan rancor and cultural cleavages. One "side" seems to view the press as the "enemy of the people," as President Trump has frequently suggested, while the other "side" sees it as beyond reproach. The truth, as usual, lies somewhere in-between. The institutional press is necessary to self-government, dissent, and democracy. But like the other institutions of democracy, it is also deeply flawed.

Since at least the American Revolution, freedom of the press has been associated with several fundamental democratic functions. As the institutional press enters a uniquely challenging era, it is appropriate to revisit these. Relatedly, we ought to think about why, despite its flaws, we must fight to preserve a free and independent press. For one thing, we do not protect constitutional rights only when and to the extent they are perfectly or even responsibly exercised. Think, for example, of the freedom of speech. So too with the institutional press, whose excesses and biases ought not to be used as grounds to eradicate a core democratic institution.

As discussed, during certain eras the Supreme Court, although it did not recognize special press rights, frequently highlighted the virtues of a free and independent press. Here is just a sample of its statements on the democratic and other functions of a free press:

- "'An untrammeled press [is] a vital source of public information,'... and an informed public is the essence of working democracy."[53]
- "In a society in which each individual has but limited time and resources with which to observe at first hand the operations of his government, he relies necessarily upon the press to bring to him in convenient form the facts of those operations."[54]
- "Without the information provided by the press most of us and many of our representatives would be unable to vote intelligently or to register opinions on the administration of government generally."[55]
- The press is "a mighty catalyst in awakening public interest in governmental affairs"[56] and an entity "specifically selected" by the Constitution "to play an important role in the discussion of public affairs."[57]
- A free press "plays a unique role as a check on government abuse."[58]
- The press "will often serve as an important restraint on government."[59]

- "The press serves and was designed to serve as a powerful antidote to any abuses of power by governmental officials and as a constitutionally chosen means for keeping officials elected by the people responsible to all the people whom they were selected to serve."[60]
- "The press has exerted a freedom in canvassing the merits and measures of public men, of every description."[61]

Many of these statements were made during what Professor RonNell Jones has described as the press's "Glory Days."[62] The Court then associated a free and independent press with educative, dialog-facilitating, and checking functions that are critical to a well-functioning democracy. Thus, the institutional press gathers and distributes vitally important information that helps inform the public about matters of public concern. It sparks and facilitates conversations and debates concerning such matters. As what Justice Stewart called a "Fourth Estate," the press checks governmental abuse of power. It exposes wrongdoing, corruption, and other kinds of misfeasance or malfeasance by elected and appointed officials.

These functions are all critically important to American democracy and to a variety of related First Amendment functions, among them facilitating citizen self-government, the pursuit of truth, and effective dissent. In order to perform these functions, the press must be free from governmental efforts to interfere with its editorial discretion. It must be able to attend important public events, such as White House briefings and criminal trials, that inform the public's understanding of democratic institutions and processes. Perhaps most important, the press must be free within broad parameters to publish information about the conduct of government officials. This must necessarily include the right to publish some information that the government would prefer to keep secret. Press exposés on government corruption, the conduct or misconduct of war, and even criminal wrongdoing by officials have facilitated self-government, dissent, and democratic change.[63] Depending on how it unfolds, the Assange prosecution may undermine a fundamental check on government abuse.

Protecting the press's right to publish has hardly been uncontroversial. The press has sometimes been viewed and treated as a dangerous institution—particularly, although not exclusively, during times of war and national conflict when publications have broadcast dissenting views that were seen as undermining national unity. Further, the institutional press has long engaged in activities that the subjects find deeply invasive and offensive. During the Trump Era, these sentiments have reached a fever pitch, with the president leading the charge by telling the American people (and people around the world) that the press is "phony," fake," and the "enemy of the people." These labels attend any coverage the president does not approve of, or that is insufficiently fawning.

Despite its abuses of trust and power, the institutional press has always been afforded a degree of latitude owing to its critical democratic functions. As the Court observed in *New York Times Co. v. Sullivan*, the "central meaning of the First Amendment" is that government cannot stifle criticism of those in power even, indeed especially, if the criticism is sharp and may negatively affect an official's reputation. "Some degree of abuse," the Supreme Court once observed, "is inseparable from the proper use of every thing, and in no instance is this more true than in that of the press."[64] The Court has characterized the press's role as so important that it "require[s] that the press have a free hand" notwithstanding its occasional exercise of poor judgment and its resort to "sensationalism."[65]

Realism about the costs and benefits of press freedom is a long-standing virtue of our First Amendment tradition. James Madison, the architect of the First Amendment, vigorously objected to the Sedition Act on free press grounds. But he was not blind to the excesses and abuses of the press, many of which had already become apparent. Thus, Madison observed:

> It has accordingly been decided by the practice of the States, that it is better to leave a few of its noxious branches to their luxuriant growth, than, by pruning them away, to injure the vigour of those yielding the proper fruits. And can the wisdom of this policy be doubted by any who reflect that to the press alone, chequered as it is with abuses, the world is indebted for all the triumphs which have been gained by reason and humanity over error and oppression; who reflect that to the same beneficent source the United States owe much of the lights which conducted them to the ranks of a free and independent nation, and which have improved their political system into a shape so auspicious to their happiness?[66]

Supreme Court decisions have echoed Madison's reflections on the importance of preserving a strong, if imperfect, press. For example, in *Near v. Minnesota*,[67] decided in 1931, the Court invalidated a state statute imposing a prior restraint on allegedly defamatory newspaper publications. In language that still resonates, it observed:

While reckless assaults upon public men, and efforts to bring obloquy upon those who are endeavoring faithfully to discharge official duties, exert a baleful influence and deserve the severest condemnation in public opinion, it cannot be said that this abuse is greater, and it is believed to be less, than that which characterized the period in which our institutions took shape. Meanwhile, the administration of government has become more complex, the opportunities for malfeasance and corruption have multiplied, crime has grown to most serious proportions, and the danger of its protection by unfaithful officials and of the impairment of fundamental security of life and property by criminal alliances and official neglect, emphasizes the primary need of a vigilant and courageous press, especially in the great cities.[68]

Particularly in light of current attacks on the press, Madison's and the Court's statements are worth quoting at length and considering carefully. Although written more than a century apart, the statements are linked by the central premise that notwithstanding its excesses, abuses, and biases, a free and independent press remains critically important to the democratic experiment. Madison and the Court candidly acknowledged the significant costs of allowing the press to doggedly pursue public officials. They did not ignore the flaws inherent in an institution with the power to investigate, report on, and ultimately discredit or even help depose public officials. They knew that bias (real and perceived), erroneous reporting, and other abuses are as natural in the "Fourth Estate" as are errors and abuses by the political branches of government. But as with other rights, including the freedom of speech, freedom of the press was not to be protected only when it was exercised responsibly.

Of course, the press has never been free to publish anything it wishes without consequence. Madison was responding to the Sedition Act, which imposed criminal penalties on press and other government critics. *Near* involved the "original sin" of the prior restraint, a means of suppressing criticism of public officials, which had long been considered presumptively unconstitutional. As discussed, it was not until the 1960s that the Sedition Act was formally interred. Before that period, the press was generally liable for all misstatements of fact and many other allegedly harmful publications.

Over time, owing to recognition that the benefits of a free and independent press counseled more latitude in reporting, publishing, and speaking—particularly about official activities—the First Amendment's free press and speech doctrines changed. Today, among other things, those doctrines accommodate non-intentional errors (i.e., those published without "actual malice"), the publication of sharply critical opinions about government, and the dissemination of certain confidential or secret information. Even President Adams, who had used the Sedition Act to punish his critics, had a change of heart once he was out of office. Both he and Thomas Jefferson, himself a sharp critic of the press when he was president, ultimately came around to the necessity of preserving a free and independent press.[69] Indeed, Jefferson ultimately supported a free and independent press as "the best instrument for enlightening the mind of man, and improving him as a rational, moral, and social being."[70]

Fast forward to the current era, when the president frequently complains about press coverage of himself and the administration. "We want fairness," President Trump has proclaimed. "Can't say things that are false, knowingly false, and be able to smile as money pours into your bank account. We are going to take a very, very strong look at that, and I think what the American people want to see is fairness." Defamation laws are established by the state, so the federal government cannot actually "open them up" or otherwise alter them (other than through a constitutional amendment or a general reconsideration of Supreme Court precedents). Freedom of the press could, however, be altered by the Supreme Court's interpretation of the First Amendment in specific cases or repeal of statutory protections afforded to the press. The press, fearing official repercussions, may also trim its own sails in covering government and public officials to make its reporting "fairer."

As noted, the costs of maintaining a free and independent press are both real and significant. The defamation rules that the Supreme Court ultimately established in *New York Times Co. v. Sullivan*, which protect the publication of false statements of fact about officials so long as they are not published with knowledge that they were false or reckless disregard for the truth, have been subject to criticism. Long before President Trump issued his call for "fairness," scholars complained that the "actual malice" standard did not adequately protect the reputational harms suffered by public officials and was unnecessary for the protection of a free and independent press.[71] Critics also worried that the defamation standards deter qualified candidates from entering the political arena.

At the same time, others argued that the standards do not go *far enough* in terms of protecting the rights of defamation defendants—in particular the institutional media.[72] Some believe that under these standards, it is still too easy to subject the press to expensive and perhaps ruinous lawsuits. As noted earlier, press defendants currently lose a higher percentage of defamation cases than they did during earlier eras and may not be financially able to defend themselves in some instances.

Debating the costs and benefits of the First Amendment defamation standards is a healthy and worthwhile democratic exercise. Prior proponents of what the president calls "fairness" have pointed to making it easier to recover certain types of damages or adopting alternative remedies for defamation such as prompt retractions or apologies. These proposals were not intended to make it easier to quash critical opinions of government or government officials, or to sue the press for millions of dollars. Rather, they were serious efforts to reckon with the balance of interests implicated when the press reports facts about governmental operations, policies, or individuals.

The argument that a powerful press, which can operate as a check on government, itself merits a degree of checking is worth considering. For the reasons discussed earlier, the press is not as powerful as the president and others would have the people believe. But despite its overall fragility, the institutional press retains a significant degree of power and influence in politics and culture. In the current news environment, the press is bound to make many mistakes as it seeks to report on matters that develop in seconds rather than days or "news cycles." It is thus wise to anticipate and reckon with those errors, as well as with the broader direction of news reporting in a fractured digital media landscape.

Reckoning with these issues requires framing them in an honest and useful way. The president's "fairness" argument differs from previous debates in two critical respects. First, it appears to be aimed at the general suppression of critical *opinions* of himself and the government, rather than at the narrower class of careless or even intentionally false factual reporting. Second, the president appears to want to use the excesses and errors of the institutional press not as a reason to "open up" the defamation standards, but rather as grounds for scrapping the institution altogether.

The president views the press as an "enemy" with which he and the American people are at "war." He sees only the costs of the press's freedom and independence. The words and context of the president's "fairness" complaint, which includes all the other threats and retaliatory measures he has taken against critics, suggest a desire to alter the rules such that the press

is compelled to project a more positive perception of the president himself and his administration. Viewed in this light, "fairness" is part of the
broader agenda to weaken and undermine the freedom and independence
of dissenters.

President Trump should be careful what he wishes for, particularly
with regard to the First Amendment's defamation standards. As discussed
earlier, the First Amendment standards that apply to the press apply as well
to individual speakers—including government officials. Surely the president knows this much, as he has been and is currently a defendant in some
defamation lawsuits. Given his penchant for public commentary on private
citizens, public figures, and public officials, more than most Americans the
president stands to benefit from current First Amendment standards.

Of course, personal liabilities and motives ought not to drive consideration of defamation standards and other press limits. Despite its flaws and
failings, the institutional press continues to be a critical bulwark against
oppressive forms of government. Realism about press freedom and a
healthy skepticism of reporting are essential elements of a self-governing
democracy. However, as Madison, Adams, Jefferson, and others long ago
realized, without a free and independent press democracy itself cannot
survive.

The "Central Meaning" of the First Amendment

The Supreme Court has observed that the "central meaning" of the First
Amendment's free speech and press guarantees is that citizens must be
free to communicate and receive facts and opinions about their government. The Trump Era poses several notable challenges to this central First
Amendment concern, particularly as it relates to the institutional press. As
discussed, these challenges come not just from the statements and policies
of governments and public officials, but from things such as market forces,
changing judicial attitudes, diminishing public support for the press, and
the manner in which people engage with news on matters of public concern.

To serve its educative and other democratic functions, the press must
be both free *and* independent—free to report on matters of public concern
and independent from government officials who would coopt and censor it.
Effective self-government depends largely on this free flow of information.
Reporting honestly and aggressively on matters of public concern facilitates

the public sharing of information, which is critical to both consent to government and dissent from it.

Tearing down the existing First Amendment defamation rules for the purpose of ensuring a more complimentary or supine press would be a step toward eradicating the press as a democratic institution. As Justice Douglas once observed, "The dominant purpose of the First Amendment was to prohibit the widespread practice of governmental suppression of embarrassing information."[73]

More broadly, the president's self-proclaimed "war" on the press poses an existential threat to the existence of a free and independent press. His threats to revoke broadcast licenses, increase postal rates for media owners, punish the press for publishing truthful information lawfully obtained, and take other retaliatory measures all raise very serious First Amendment concerns. Even if they are intended to produce media self-censorship rather than official acts of retribution, we ought to be concerned about this chilling effect.

A recent conflict sheds light on the nature of current challenges. Sparring with or even criticizing reporters has long been a normal part of press–president interaction. But engaging in acts of retaliation and threatening to use executive power to punish journalists or media outlets based on their coverage are not normal. When the press secretary revoked the "hard pass" issued to a CNN reporter after the reporter engaged in a tense back and forth with President Trump at a presidential news conference, another norm relating to press freedoms was breached. The president argued in court that he had *absolute discretion* to engage with whichever reporters he chose, presumably for any reason.

As we know, the press is not entitled to access to briefings or press passes. However, once access has been provided, revoking press credentials or excluding reporters on the basis of their negative coverage or the content of their questions implicates First Amendment free press and speech rights.[74] I say "implicates" because there is very little case law concerning whether this action would violate the First Amendment. The lack of precedent is itself testament to the unusual nature of the action taken. Whether this episode or others like it violate the First Amendment, such actions cut against long-standing norms relating to press access to and questioning of government officials. They also serve as an official warning to reporters and the press that "disrespectful" or critical questioning of government officials will lead to professional reprisals.

Of course, as noted earlier, presidents have long had tense relationships with pamphleteers, newspapers, and other media. George Washington characterized the press as "infamous scribblers." During his presidency, Thomas Jefferson wrote in private correspondence that "[n]othing can now be believed which is seen in a newspaper." "Truth itself," he complained, "becomes suspicious by being put into that polluted vehicle."[75] As discussed, the First Congress authorized criminal prosecutions of government critics, and many publishers went to jail as a result. Presidents from Adams to Nixon have had many unkind things to say about the press, mostly in private conversations and correspondence. President Obama's administration was also sharply criticized, in particular for issuing subpoenas to reporters for information about confidential sources.

A student of history might say that things have indeed been much worse. Under the Sedition Act, publishers were actually thrown in jail for their critical coverage. However, that era is hardly an appropriate benchmark for modern free press and free speech principles. Indeed, it was the impetus for the Supreme Court's articulation of the First Amendment's "central meaning."

For a few reasons, the contemporary "war" on the press is historically distinct. President Trump's public, vitriolic, and incessant peacetime campaign to discredit the media has no historical analog. As noted earlier, no president has ever publicly referred to the press, as President Trump has on several occasions, as "the enemy of the American people." This goes beyond criticizing news coverage or purported professional lapses. It suggests that the institutional press is not just untrustworthy, but illegitimate and unpatriotic—a force of evil aligned against the interests of the United States and its people. Similarly, the president's public attacks on individual reporters and journalists suggest that members of the institutional press are personal enemies, to be heckled or perhaps even physically harmed.

Further, the "war" the president is waging is not only a war on the press but also a war on fact and truth itself. As the president understands it, "fake news" is not manufactured reporting, but rather any news that does not fit the administration's own narrative. In this war, "alternative facts" are being used as countermeasures in an attempt to destroy even things we can all see with our own eyes. As President Trump once said to a rally audience, "What you're seeing and what you're reading is not what's happening."

Press Preservation

The war on the media and the broader battle for "truth" itself are serious threats to the press and public discourse. Engaging and fighting in this "war" will be critical to the preservation of the press.

However, we need to also recognize that the media is partly to blame for the current predicament. There is no small irony in the president's strategy to undermine the credibility of the institutional press. That institution arguably played a singular role in creating the Trump phenomenon, in part by granting the campaign and now the administration massive amounts of free media. A new dysfunctional symbiosis has emerged, one in which the media rely on Trump to create content that draws viewers and readers and the president simultaneously conducts his "war" on the press for political gain.

Thus, how the media responds to the press war of the Trump Era will help to determine its own future. It will have to defend not only its First Amendment rights, but also its public credibility. The war on truth has been facilitated by a media landscape in which partisans look to favored outlets for news and information and distrust all other sources. This makes the sort of rational debate that a free and independent press ought to facilitate next to impossible. Contestants in debates cannot even agree on the underlying facts relating to policies concerning matters such as immigration, national security, and healthcare. The media does no service to democratic discourse when it falsely equates things or positions that are not equal, broadcasts lies in order to "balance" its coverage, or breathlessly parses presidential tweets to the exclusion of news relating to matters of public concern.

It will be difficult to break free of these practices. Market and economic concerns will continue to drive coverage to some degree. The media landscape will likely remain fractured. However, past efforts to suppress criticism and truth-seeking have left us with some important lessons. For instance, historians have observed that even in the face of Sedition Act prosecutions, reporting on governmental excess and misconduct not only "continued unabated, but intensified."[76] Like our colonial forebears, modern media must not capitulate to official demands to silence criticism or shade investigative reporting to suit official or public narratives. It must push back against efforts to retaliate against reporters for performing their checking function and to undermine the notion of a free press.

Fighting back is important, but it will not be enough. As public opinion polling shows, the long "war" on media credibility, which began long before the Trump presidency but has now reached a fever pitch, has taken a substantial toll in terms of the media's trust and reputation. The institutional media will have to do more than provide critical coverage and incessant fact-checking of public officials. If it is to survive its current financial, technological, and other challenges, the institutional press will need to be more resilient and creative.[77] Sound-bite reporting, tweet-reading, and scandal-mongering are not going to restore public confidence in the media.

As the past few years have demonstrated, constantly reacting to every public statement the president makes is a pernicious trap. It obscures issues and concerns outside the Twitter timeline, which affect real people and actual lives. Moreover, the media's treatment of governance as entertainment has not benefitted a public that knows less and less about the actual workings of its own government. As educators and discourse-initiators, the media must develop and nurture markets for news and information that can provide potential antidotes to partisan truth-splicing. There is a market for this kind of coverage, and some media outlets do already provide it. But it is not nearly enough. Without such efforts, it is possible that more and more Americans might conclude that the costs of having a free press outweigh its social and political benefits.

History also shows that the institutional press will not be able to save itself or survive on its own. When it comes to the preservation of a free and independent press, there are many stakeholders. Legislators, who may themselves need to be educated about the actual meaning of the Press Clause and the fragility of the modern press, have a role to play. They can enact and preserve legal protections that allow the press to function, including laws that protect reporters' sources from being disclosed. Despite changes to the government–press dynamic, most lawmakers still rely on the press to disseminate news of their accomplishments and to inform their constituencies about public issues. Self-interest and the broader public interest ought to lead to a more protective legislative agenda regarding the institutional press.

Courts also need to reconnect with the lessons of the "Glory Days," when the democratic functions of the institutional press were articulated and defended (even if such defenses did not lead to "special" rights) despite the press's known excesses. Even if the Supreme Court is not going to adopt a more "institutional" conception of the Press Clause or recognize "special" press rights, its decisions on press-related rights such as newsgathering can help to preserve a free and independent press. The Court can also return to its tradition of recognizing and articulating the democratic benefits associated with freedom of the press. In their decisions and public remarks, judges can educate the public about the traditions and functions of a free press.

With regard to the fate of a free and independent press, the people themselves obviously have the most to gain or lose. Activists will remain committed to governmental transparency and other principles that facilitate the free and open distribution of information about government. However, in a broader sense, the people bear significant responsibility for preserving a free and independent press.

For far too long, we have allowed ourselves to fall prey to partisan impulses when it comes to news consumption. Some have become too lazy to be skeptical about the news they receive or its sourcing. Others have become too skeptical of anything presenting itself as "news," viewing it mostly as false or "fake" if it does not confirm their own biases. Still others have effectively outsourced credibility determinations to favored outlets, pundits, or officials, effectively allowing them to determine what is "fake" and what is "real."

It may not be possible to return to a time when a significant majority of Americans trusted and felt positively about the institutional media. But there is one critical respect in which the First Amendment doctrines of speech and press coincide with the realities of self-government. As discussed earlier, the First Amendment protects the rights of *all* individuals to collect, disseminate, and consume information. These rights belong to, and need to be exercised by, the people.

We do not need media to filter or characterize the news. However, we do need it to help provide the information necessary for us to make self-governing choices. Our responsibilities, as citizens, are first to become more astute and critical consumers of information and then to teach future generations how to critically analyze news sources and separate fact from fiction. In sum, realizing the "central meaning" of the First Amendment is not solely a project for the press. It is an undertaking we must all participate in, as stewards of our First Amendment free speech and press traditions.

Should this mission fail, the harms and consequences are likely to be dire. A recent poll found that more than 40 percent of self-identified Republicans would give the president the power to shut down certain media outlets "engaged in bad behavior."[78] That would be the act of an autocrat, not the leader of an established democracy with a free and independent press. It would vest in government the dangerous power to quash dissent.

The stakes for individual reporters are also critical. According to the Committee to Protect Journalists, an advocacy group that does an annual count of detained and killed journalists across the globe, in 2018 at least 48 journalists have been killed on the job. In many cases, the journalists were performing the press's central checking function. Saudi Arabian officials have been accused of plotting and carrying out the murder of Jamaal Khashoggi, a prominent Saudi critic who contributed to *The Washington Post*. Bulgarian authorities are investigating the rape and murder of Viktoria Marinova, an investigative reporter. In October 2017, Maltese investigative journalist Daphne Caruana Galizia was killed by a car bomb near her home. She was working on the so-called Panama Papers, leaked documents that revealed financial information about the offshore accounts of high-profile officials.

Reporters face the threat of death in the United States as well, although not directly at the hands of public officials. A man was recently arrested after he referred to several reporters working at the *Boston Globe* as "the enemy of the people" and threatened to harm them. In June 2018, five journalists who worked for the *Capital Gazette* in Annapolis, Maryland, were shot by a man who had a grievance against the paper, stemming from an unsuccessful defamation lawsuit he filed against it.

Whether these incidents are directly linked to the president's statements is largely beside the point. Regardless of whether there is a demonstrable causal connection, the president's rhetoric of "war" against an "enemy" press responsible for spreading "fake" news must be taken seriously. This is not the discourse of a responsible leader aware of the democratic values of a free and independent press. It is the misuse of the bully pulpit by a would-be authoritarian intent on discrediting that institution in an effort to convince the people that truth emanates from only one source—himself.

The press is in trouble—even in democratic nations where leaders do not resort to official censorship or murder. Right-wing populist parties are seeking to undermine the credibility of the press in a number of European Union nations. Reporters have been jailed or subject to government intimidation in Bulgaria, Slovakia, Romania, Serbia, and Montenegro. The ruling party in nominally democratic Hungary has recently published lists of "enemy" journalists. Despite the existence of constitutional protections for freedom of the press and freedom of speech, Hungary's legal environment has grown increasingly hostile to opposition newspapers and the free distribution of information.

Across the world, the combination of media consolidation, revenue loss, attacks on individual reporters, financial and other forms of retaliation against press outlets, and the labeling of the press as "the enemy of the people" now threatens the very existence of a free and independent press. We should not pretend that these trends have nothing to do with the "wars" now being waged on the press and the truth in the United States. The world is watching. Historically, constitutionally, and institutionally, America is better-situated than most nations to resist such threats. However, as recent events here and abroad have made clear, Americans cannot simply take a free and independent press for granted.

In response to a question about what the Founders had created in Philadelphia in 1787, a republic or a monarchy, Benjamin Franklin reportedly responded "a republic . . . if you can keep it."[79] Like the republic itself, the continued existence of a free and independent press is not guaranteed. And history demonstrates that the survival of one is indelibly linked to the fate of the other.

2

Sedition

*If we advert to the nature of Republican Government, we shall find
that the censorial power is in the people over the Government, and not
in the Government over the people.*[1]

Throughout American history, governments have sought to suppress "sedition." "Sedition" has been defined in different ways—as defamation of government and public officials in 1798, as incitement to insurrection during World War I, and as "disloyalty" during the twentieth century's Red Scare eras. However defined, what the different conceptions share in common is their use as a means of suppressing expression that is critical of government or official policies.

As noted in chapter 1, it wasn't until the 1960s that the Supreme Court formally rejected the crime of "seditious libel" as fundamentally incompatible with the "central meaning of the First Amendment."[2] James Madison had reached that conclusion much earlier, when he observed in the context of the debate over the Sedition Act that in a democracy the "censorial power" belongs to the people and not to the government.

The Trump Era has once again focused attention on the locus of "censorial power" and sedition. The president has suggested that the expression of criticism or negative viewpoints about government or the president himself are "seditious." Indeed, as in prior eras, charges of sedition saturate our political discourse, with supporters of the president charging that opponents are guilty of sedition, subversion, disloyalty, or treason. Unlike prior eras, however, the concern with sedition does not relate to the conduct of war or threats to our national security. The principal loyalty at issue is not to the United States or its causes, but to the person of the president.

In the present era, no one has (yet) advocated the revival of the crime of "seditious libel"—jailing or punishing speakers for criticizing government officials. However, the president has suggested punishing or retaliating

The First Amendment in the Trump Era. Timothy Zick.
© Timothy Zick 2019. Published 2019 by Oxford University Press.

against government critics, including members of the institutional press, former government officials, and even White House advisors. President Trump appears to see sedition lurking in many places—including in satirical comedy shows and Google's search algorithm, both of which he has advocated "looking into" on the ground that they disseminate negative information about him. These statements may merely be among the many incendiary things the president says in order to drive the news cycle or animate his political base. However, they may instead foreshadow the president's use of emergency and other powers, which have been granted under federal laws, to silence critics or even alter algorithmic search results.[3]

The First Amendment lessons relating to sedition go back a long way. We will spend some time in this chapter reviewing the historical record. Among other things, that record will show that things have sometimes been much worse for critics of government. Many were jailed for publishing "seditious" material. We no longer have criminal sedition laws. However, one of the important lessons of history that now applies to the First Amendment in the Trump Era is that the suppression of "seditious" communications takes many forms, all of which pose serious dangers to dissent and democracy. The new sedition, like the old, threatens to chill reporting and commentary (even comedic or satiric versions) relating to the functions of government. Another lesson is that the people and democratic institutions cannot always be relied upon to preserve the right to dissent. The Trump Era reminds us that like a free and independent press, the right to dissent is not guaranteed but earned through vigilance and constant activism.

Sedition, Subversion, and Disloyalty in the Trump Era

As we will see, in various historical eras sedition and disloyalty have been subject to direct forms of criminal punishment. The United States has enacted and enforced two Sedition Acts, one in 1798 and the other in 1918. It has taken many other measures to suppress criticism and dissent, particularly during times of war and international conflict.

There are a number of less direct ways to limit or control the expression of public criticism and dissent. For example, governments have regulated and manipulated public space in order to marginalize dissenters.[4] By sharply limiting access to public officials, spatial regulations and tactics can diminish opportunities to communicate dissenting points of view. The First Amendment scholar Ronald Krotoszynski describes efforts to limit access to public officials as the "new seditious libel."[5] Trump Era limits of this nature will be discussed in chapter 4, which considers limits on speech in public places. This chapter will generally define sedition as criticism of government or public officials, and will be primarily concerned with the punishment or chilling of such expression.

Although we do not currently have a Sedition Act, the president has indeed punished some of his critics. For example, he revoked the security clearance of former CIA director John Brennan—apparently in retaliation for Brennan's public criticisms of the president and his policies.[6] President Trump has vowed to do the same thing to other government officials. As noted in chapter 1, he has also threatened to use federal antitrust and tax laws to punish Amazon, owing again to critical statements that its owner Jeff Bezos has made about the administration and President Trump. These measures implicate both press freedoms and the free speech right to criticize government.

As we will see, accusations of "sedition" and "disloyalty" are common in American political discourse. Some of President Trump's political supporters have characterized media and public criticism of the Trump administration as "seditious" or even "treasonous." These advocates are referring not to conduct or concrete acts that threaten or undermine the government or the interests of the nation, but to the expression of criticism of the president himself or his policies.President Trump has openly encouraged this perspective. For instance, as discussed in chapter 1, he has frequently referred to the media as "the enemy of the American people." In this way, the president has facilitated the (false) equation of public criticism with sedition, subversion, and disloyalty.

In addition to the significant harms to free speech and self-government, there are physical risks associated with treating critics as "enemies." A man was arrested for repeatedly threatening *Boston Globe* reporters after accusing them, based on their critical coverage of President Trump, of "sedition" and of being the "enemy of the people."

Charges of sedition have not been reserved for the media. When a self-described senior advisor anonymously published a critical account of the Trump administration in the *New York Times*, one of the president's former advisors described the publication and its content as a "confession of sedition." Publication of the op-ed would likely be grounds for termination.

Had the op-ed revealed secret or confidential information, the author might have been arrested for violating federal laws. Otherwise, the First Amendment protects publication of the op-ed, unless it is intended to and likely will result in imminent unlawful action.[7]

But the op-ed did not advocate any crime. It conveyed embarrassing information about the president and the manner in which the Trump administration operates. President Trump encouraged the Department of Justice to investigate anyway. That course would only be appropriate if the Department determined that a crime had been committed. He also argued, as have previous officials faced with criticisms, that the op-ed created a national security concern. President Trump publicly opined that the *New York Times* should disclose the identity of the author or "turn him over" for investigation and possible prosecution. The president also suggested that the *New York Times* itself should be investigated for merely publishing the op-ed—again, an act the First Amendment undoubtedly protects.[8]

Pursuit of "seditious" speakers and publishers is consistent with the administration's general reaction to all forms of public criticism. The president has publicly conceded that he takes such criticism "personally." This may explain why he has reportedly required administration officials to sign nondisclosure agreements that prohibit them from criticizing Trump, his businesses, and the administration more generally. These agreements, which appear to be unprecedented in the history of the executive branch, are intended to suppress or discourage the communication or publication of criticism of government and individuals working in government. In this respect, they too are modern-day "sedition" measures.

Even search engines and comedy shows may have something to fear from the current administration. President Trump has publicly suggested that federal regulators "look into" the algorithm Google uses to return search results. He claims, without any evidence, that the algorithm discriminates by suppressing conservative views and, more importantly, favoring stories that make the president "look bad."[9] The president has described this as "a very serious situation" and promised that it "will be addressed!" The Director of the National Economic Council later confirmed that the White House was indeed "taking a look at" whether Google's search engine should be regulated in some fashion. President Trump has even suggested that the comedy sketch show *Saturday Night Live* "should be investigated" for its parodies of the president.

The point of "investigating" Google or a Saturday night comedy show is not entirely clear. The president and his advisors might be suggesting a "balancing" of search results or satire that would result in more "good" stories making it to the top of the list or more flattering comedy sketches. But the First Amendment prohibits the government from mandating balanced results or any "right of reply." It also forbids cancelling broadcast licenses for satiric criticism of government.[10] In other words, Google cannot be forced to alter its algorithm in ways that are more complimentary to or less critical of the president or conservative ideas generally. And the government cannot require *Saturday Night Live* to pull its punches or water down its presidential parodies. All this may be cold comfort to Google and network broadcasters, however, who may rationally fear being "looked at" or investigated by federal regulators .

As we will see, the prosecution of "sedition" has long been associated with allegations of "disloyalty." Part of the reason for this connection relates to the fact that sedition has historically been treated as an acute problem during wartime, when governments arguably have a strong interest in national unity. However, history also demonstrates that charges of "disloyalty" have generally been false or unsubstantiated, and that the persecution of "disloyal" Americans has greatly harmed both the subject individuals and our democracy.

In the Trump Era, nationalistic themes seem to fit hand in glove with official demands for "loyalty." As discussed in chapter 3, the president's "America First" policies and his focus on patriotic expression are part of an effort to impose a patriotic orthodoxy. However, in the Trump Era, demands for "loyalty" seem to relate not to the nation but primarily to the president himself. In contrast to other eras, when disloyalty was considered a threat to the nation owing to its effect on the conduct of war, the Trump Era has been one of relative international peace. The president's insistence on nondisclosure agreements, his desire for pledges of loyalty from government officials, and the personal disfavor he and supporters have shown to individuals who are considered "disloyal" all suggest a concept of "sedition" that focuses on a personal brand of loyalty to the person of the president.

To be sure, none of these statements and actions rise to the level of prosecuting and jailing governmental critics. In contrast to past eras, the government has not (yet) established loyalty boards to ferret out and investigate "disloyal" individuals. Presidents are allowed to express frustration with criticisms and leaks. They are even entitled to a degree of personal loyalty from their advisors—although one would hope that officials' ultimate loyalties are to the people they serve.

However, executive actions are on much shakier First Amendment ground when they take the form of sanctions imposed on critics. What has come before is a warning of what may happen again—particularly if the people, the courts, and government officials succumb to the sort of partisanship and hysteria that has characterized past anti-sedition programs. For this reason, it is critically important that we recall important historical lessons relating to sedition, dissent, and democracy.

Seditious Libel in Early America

In colonial America, publishing or communicating material that "defamed" government or brought it into disrepute was a serious crime. Before 1700, there were more than a thousand prosecutions involving allegedly seditious publications. The penalties included confinement to the stocks, public whippings, and much worse. For example, a Massachusetts offender had his ears cut off for criticizing government officials. A Virginia offender had his tongue pierced with an awl. He actually got off easy—under Virginia's laws at the time, criticizing the governor was a crime punishable by death.

Things ended on a brighter note for some accused of "seditious libel." Students of early American history are likely familiar with the 1735 trial of New York printer John Peter Zenger. Zenger, a German immigrant, was sued by Britain's royal governor of New York and New Jersey, William Cosby, for the crime of "seditious libel."[11] Zenger's newspaper had accused the colonial government of rigging elections and allowing the French enemy to explore New York harbor. The paper had also published stories that the governor had committed a variety of crimes. The authors of these pieces remained anonymous. Zenger was arrested and jailed for publishing them.

Under colonial "seditious libel" law, defendants were not permitted to argue the truth of their statements as a defense. In fact, since it further undermined the government's authority, truth actually exacerbated the harm of seditious libel. The jury's task was simply to decide whether the offending matter had been printed. The judge's role was then to decide whether the statements damaged the person's reputation. Since Zenger did not deny printing the articles in question and the judge was likely to find that they damaged Cosby's reputation, a verdict against Zenger was sure to follow. However, as students of history and the First Amendment know, the jurors famously refused to convict and Zenger was set free.

The Zenger verdict was a shot across the bow to colonial officials who thought they could rely on suppressing dissent to assure the people's loyalty. The prosecution did not deter colonial publishers. Indeed, as historians have noted, publication of critical accounts of government officials and policies was crucial to the success of the American Revolution.[12] Radical newspapers regularly criticized the British prime minister as well as local colonial officials. Although it remained on the books, the crime of "seditious libel" was buried under an avalanche of public criticism of the Stamp Act of 1765 and other measures many colonists vehemently opposed. Jurors, largely sympathetic to the arguments presented in broadsides, cartoons, and other publications, often refused to convict.

Freedom of speech and freedom of press were expressly included in what ended up being the First Amendment to the U.S. Constitution (in fact, it was third on the original list, and only ended up first because two prior proposals were defeated). Scholars and historians have long debated whether the ratification of the First Amendment was intended to abolish the crime of "seditious libel." After all, those who framed and ratified the free speech and press provisions were aware of the history of "seditious libel" prosecutions during the colonial and Revolutionary eras. That same experience also demonstrated the importance of free speech and press to effective self-government.

Whatever the Founders may have intended, the crime of "seditious libel" obviously survived the ratification of the First Amendment in 1791. In July 1798, the First Congress passed and President John Adams signed into law the Alien and Sedition Acts. The "Alien" part of the law allowed the government to deport immigrants and made it harder for naturalized citizens to vote. The "Sedition" part of the law made it illegal to "write, print, utter, or publish" any material "*with intent to defame the said government, or either house of the said Congress, or the said President, or to bring them, or either of them, into contempt or disrepute; or to excite against them, or either or any of them, the hatred of the good people of the United States, or to stir up sedition with the United States.*" Violation of the Sedition Act was punishable by fine not exceeding $2,000 and two years' imprisonment.

As we will see, throughout American history, "seditious" speech has been a popular target for suppression during wartime.[13] Indeed, as the First Amendment scholar Geoffrey Stone has observed: "In the entire history of the United States, the national government has never attempted to punish opposition to government policies, *except* in times of war."[14] (The Trump Era may establish an exception to this historical rule.) In 1798, the nation was preparing for a possible war with France. Thus, some supporters of the Sedition Act pointed to national security as a justification for penalizing "seditious" matter. One way to assure support for war with France was to suppress dissent that might undermine the war effort.

However, as historians have observed, there were also clear partisan motives for the adoption and enforcement of the Sedition Act. Scholars have debated whether President Adams personally supported the sedition provision as a means of silencing his critics, or whether the Federalist Party in Congress pressured him to support it. Whatever the case, the law was indeed used to silence supporters of the opposition Democratic-Republican Party led by Thomas Jefferson, who was then the vice president. As the Sedition Act was aggressively enforced against the administration's critics, Adams did not exhibit any reluctance or regret. Many of his strongest critics were fined and jailed for publishing personal attacks on Adams's character and his presidency.

James Callender, a pro-Jefferson journalist for the *Richmond Examiner*, wrote an election campaign pamphlet that said of Adams: "As President he has never opened his lips, or lifted his pen, without threatening and scolding; the grand object of his administration has been to exasperate the rage of contending parties . . . and destroy every man who differs from his opinions." Based on this publication, Callender was convicted of "seditious libel," fined $200 and sent to federal prison for nine months. Undeterred, he wrote from his prison cell that Adams was "a gross hypocrite and an unprincipled oppressor." In 1800, Thomas Cooper, editor of the *Northumberland Gazette* in Pennsylvania, wrote that Adams was a "power-mad despot." He too was convicted for publishing "a false, scandalous and malicious attack on the character" of President Adams with the intent "to excite the hatred and contempt of the people of this country against the man of their choice."

In 1799, Charles Holt, editor of the *New London Bee* in Connecticut, published an article accusing the Treasury secretary of seeking to establish a standing army. He also took some personal jabs at the secretary, including an implied charge of adultery. Holt was charged with being a "wicked, malicious seditious and ill-disposed person—greatly disaffected" to the U.S. government. He was fined $200 and sent to jail for three months.

As Luther Baldwin discovered, even private remarks could be the basis for "seditious libel" charges. Baldwin was passing through Newark in 1798 on his way to his summer home in Massachusetts. President Adams rode in his coach in a downtown parade, complete with a 16-cannon salute. When Baldwin and a friend heard the cannon shots while drinking heavily at a local tavern, one of them remarked: "There goes the president, and they are firing at his arse." Baldwin responded that he didn't care "if they fired thro' his arse." The tavern owner reported the conversation, and both Baldwin and his drinking buddy were fined and jailed for seditious libel.

Ultimately, more than two dozen people were convicted of "seditious libel" during the Adams administration. Public reaction to the prosecutions was mixed. While some of Adams's critics were lionized for criticizing him, others received death threats, were assaulted, or had their homes vandalized. Some of the convictions led to public protests and defenses of freedom of speech and press. James Madison argued that the press had played a vital role in defeating the British in the American Revolution. "The press has exerted a freedom in canvassing the merits and measures of public men, of every description," he wrote. "On this footing, the freedom of the press has stood; on this footing it yet stands."

Thomas Jefferson and James Madison both strongly opposed the Alien and Sedition Acts. The two statesmen wrote anonymous criticisms of the Acts, known as the Kentucky Resolution and Virginia Resolution. Jefferson's Kentucky Resolution argued that the Acts violated the states' guarantee of rights under the Constitution's Tenth Amendment, which reserves to the states or the people all powers not granted to the federal government. The Resolution called the laws "nothing short of despotism." Madison's Virginia Resolution was equally critical, but it focused not only on the lack of federal authority to enact the laws but also on their violation of the First Amendment's free speech and press provisions. The Sedition Act, Madison wrote, "exercises in like manner, a power not delegated by the Constitution . . . which *more than any other, ought to produce universal alarm, because it is levelled against that right of freely examining public characters and measures, and of free communication among the people thereon, which has ever been justly deemed, the only effectual guardian of every other right."*

President Adams and the Federalists defended their crackdown on public and private dissent. They claimed that the criticisms were intended to undermine Adams's lawful election (sound familiar?) and the government's preparations for war with France. Thomas Jefferson made opposition to the Alien and Sedition Acts a major part of his campaign in the 1800 presidential election, which he narrowly won. The Acts expired at the end of President Adams's term. Now-president Jefferson pardoned all who had been convicted under the law and refunded their fines.

Although both were offended by public criticism, Jefferson and Adams later came to appreciate the need to preserve the freedom to criticize government and its officials. In his 1801 inauguration speech, Jefferson praised the right of citizens "to think freely and to speak and write what they think." However, the Sedition Act would only be the first of many governmental efforts to suppress dissent and attempt to coerce "loyalty" to the United States.

Sedition and Disloyalty in Times of War and National Conflict

As Professor Geoffrey Stone has documented, the Adams administration may have been the first to prosecute critics of government and public officials, but it was hardly the last. In the United States, every wartime era has been punctuated by official efforts to quell or censor dissent and coerce loyalty.

During the conduct of the Civil War, President Lincoln's administration pursued and prosecuted wartime dissenters. As Professor Stone observes, in many instances suppression of dissent occurred at the direction of military and other officials and without Lincoln's direct approval or involvement. As Stone notes, "Often called a 'tyrant' for his conduct of the war, Lincoln struggled to leave unpunished even the most vicious utterances. And in those instances when he did approve the suppression of dissent, he offered thoughtful explanations of his judgments and posed serious questions about the appropriate limits of free speech in wartime."[15] Nevertheless, suppression of dissent, again under a "seditious libel" justification, was a stark reality for many during the Civil War Era.

More than a century after the Alien and Sedition Acts expired, President Woodrow Wilson proposed the Espionage Act of 1917 and, shortly after that, the Sedition Act of 1918. Unlike President Lincoln, President Wilson had little tolerance for wartime critics or dissent. Indeed, he often expressed the view that "disloyal" individuals had forfeited their civil liberties.[16]

The Espionage Act and Sedition Act prohibited communications and actions that were intended to interfere with the war effort. They criminalized speech that caused or attempted to cause "insubordination, disloyalty, mutiny, or refusal of duty, in the military or naval forces of the United States." The laws also criminalized efforts to "obstruct or attempt to obstruct the recruiting or enlistment services of the United States." Advocating, teaching, or defending such conduct was also made a crime.

The nation's second federal Sedition Act bore a strong resemblance to its first. It subjected to criminal punishment any person who "shall willfully utter, print, write or publish any *disloyal, profane, scurrilous, or abusive language about the form of government of the United States or the Constitution of the United States, or the military or naval forces of the United States, or the flag of the United States, or the uniform of the Army or Navy of the United States*" with intent to bring such things "into contempt, scorn, contumely, or disrepute." The 1918 Act also criminalized "any language intended to incite, provoke, or encourage resistance to the United States, or to promote the cause of its enemies," or the willful "display [of] the flag of any foreign enemy." As Professor Stone has described it, the Act was "the perfect instrument to suppress dissent."[17]

In truth, things could have been, and in some cases were, much worse for dissenters. During the Sedition Act debate, one senator proposed that any citizen found to be "disloyal" should lose his citizenship and forfeit all of his property.[18] (As discussed in chapter 3, President Trump has proposed a similar punishment for flag-burners.) Anti-dissent fervor was high and mob violence against those suspected of disloyalty was common. Indeed, in 1918, an Illinois man was hanged on suspicion of disloyalty.[19] Public vigilante violence supplemented legal proscriptions on allegedly "seditious" and "disloyal" expression. The people acted as an informal, but alarmingly effective, censor.

The Espionage Act (which remains in effect today) and the Sedition Act (which lapsed in 1921) were invoked against a variety of politically unpopular wartime dissidents and political speakers—socialists, communists, pacifists, and anarchists. States also got into the act, with several adopting sedition laws and other restrictions on "disloyal" expression. Interpreting these laws during a period of wartime hysteria, courts and juries generally embraced a narrow interpretation of freedom of speech and press under which government was allowed to censor antiwar dissent. During this repressive era, speakers and publishers who merely "questioned the legality, morality, or conduct of the war" were convicted and sent to prison.[20]

In 1919, the Supreme Court heard a series of challenges to prosecutions under the Espionage Act and Sedition Act. This was the Court's first substantive engagement with the First Amendment. In decisions upholding all of the convictions, the Court held that the First Amendment did not prevent the government from punishing communications that posed a "clear and present danger" to national interests.[21] In truth, the danger in these cases was hardly "clear" and never "present." Most of the communications and publications found to be unlawful amounted to little more than strong criticism of the war, the draft, and foreign policy. One pamphlet the Court reviewed compared the draft to slavery, while another criticized U.S. war efforts in Russia owing to their effect on the revolution there. Although none of the communications posed any real or imminent danger to the war effort, they were the basis for lengthy prison terms.

The 1919 cases resurrected debates about the constitutionality of the 1798 Sedition Act. In the World War I cases, the Court viewed the communications and publications as going beyond mere dissent or criticism of government. However, in a dissent that presaged a more robust future interpretation of First Amendment rights, Justice Oliver Wendell Holmes Jr. (joined by Justice Louis Brandeis) saw nothing in the pamphlets or communications that posed any actual danger to the war effort. "In this case," he observed, "sentences of twenty years' imprisonment have been imposed for the publishing of two leaflets that I believe the defendants had as much right to publish as the Government has to publish the Constitution of the United States now vainly invoked by them."[22] With regard to punishment for "sedition," Holmes wrote, "I wholly disagree with the argument of the Government that the First Amendment left the common law as to seditious libel in force. History seems to me against the notion. I had conceived that the United States, through many years, had shown its repentance for the Sedition Act of 1798, by repaying fines that it imposed."[23]

Like other Holmes dissents, this one turned out to be prescient. However, before its promise could be realized, thousands of speakers and publishers were convicted and jailed—most under the Espionage Act.

In the immediate aftermath of World War I, the nation plunged straightaway into the Red Scare of 1919–1920. After the success of the Russian revolution, Russians and radicals were cast as the new "enemies of the people." After a series of violent labor strikes in the United States, officials pointed the finger at socialists, communists, and anarchists. The nation was at war with radicalism and communism—this time at home.

The U.S. Attorney General, A. Mitchell Palmer, publicly crusaded against radicalism, used dragnets to round up aliens suspected of radical activities, and deported thousands. Also during this era, two-thirds of the states enacted laws prohibiting the advocacy of criminal anarchy and criminal syndicalism—in essence, the idea that organized government should be overthrown by force, violence, or other unlawful means. The laws went much further than this in terms of suppressing dissent. They criminalized a range of "disloyal" communications, including the display of a Red flag as a symbol of opposition to government.[24]

Challenges to anti-syndicalism laws would ultimately reach the Supreme Court. Although the Court seemed to take the First Amendment arguments more seriously this time, it upheld the convictions all the same. States had jailed speakers for giving speeches, circulating "manifestos," and joining groups that advocated a "Communist Revolution" through class struggle, mobilization of the proletariat, political strikes, and industrial revolts. Although the publications, speeches, and associations were not linked to any violence or other dangerous effects, the Supreme Court allowed the convictions to stand.[25]

It did so over the objections of Justices Brandeis and Holmes, who argued that the speech and publications amounted to political speech that the states could only criminalize in the case of some actual and imminent emergency. Justice Brandeis explained: "Fear of serious injury cannot alone justify suppression of free speech and assembly. Men feared witches and burned women. . . . To justify suppression of free speech there must be reasonable ground to fear that serious evil will result if free speech is practiced."[26] Brandeis and Holmes were of the view that only a "clear and present danger" of "immediate serious violence" constituted valid grounds for suppressing expression.[27] As Brandeis observed, "If there be time to expose through discussion the falsehood and fallacies, to avert the evil by the processes of education, the remedy to be applied is more speech, not enforced silence. Only an emergency can justify repression."[28]

Brandeis and Holmes failed to convince a majority of the Court to adopt their approach to "clear and present danger." As a result, speakers and publishers were prosecuted and convicted for advocating or teaching what were essentially political ideologies. Courts largely deferred to legislative judgments that such ideologies, though generally rejected by the people, threatened the government's existence.

During a "Second Red Scare," which lasted from the late 1940s through the 1950s, government officials again set their sights on communists and radicals. Fears relating to the Soviet Union's recent successful testing of an atomic bomb, as well as the rise of fascism within the United States, generated new restrictions on seditious and subversive expression. Senator Joseph McCarthy of Wisconsin became the official face of American anti-communism. Through hearings of the House Un-American Activities Committee, Senator McCarthy leveled unfounded accusations of subversion and treason against government employees, celebrities, academics, and others in an effort to expel them from government, the academy, and society. This gave rise to the term "McCarthyism," which was associated with the making of demagogic and unsubstantiated accusations of sedition, subversion, treason, or disloyalty to country.

During the Second Red Scare, speakers and publishers were prosecuted under the Smith Act of 1940, a federal analog to the state syndicalism laws discussed earlier. States enacted their own stringent anti-communism and anti-sedition laws. Some states also conducted their own investigations of suspected communists and communist-sympathizers.

Hundreds of speakers and publishers were prosecuted under the Smith Act and state anti-communism laws, and thousands more, including military personnel, lost their jobs owing to mere accusations of communism and subversion. Once again, the First Amendment was not an effective defense.

In *Dennis v. United States*, the Supreme Court upheld the conviction under the Smith Act of a group of alleged communists. The group was accused of conspiring to associate for the purpose of advocating and teaching the duty and necessity of overthrowing the government of the United States by force or violence.[29] The Court concluded that *advocating* the tenets of Marxism-Leninism constituted a "clear and present danger" to the United States, notwithstanding a lack of evidence that the Communist Party then posed any imminent threat to the nation.

Disloyalty and Dissent

As Professor Stone has observed, "It is often said that dissent in wartime is disloyal."[30] Charges of "disloyalty" went hand in glove with prosecutions under the Sedition Act of 1798, the Espionage Act of 1917, and the Sedition Act of 1918. The vigilante activities mentioned earlier, including the hanging of the suspected disloyalist in Illinois, were also rooted in public suspicion that the targets of violence were not loyal to their country.

During the Second Red Scare, many states required their employees to sign "loyalty oaths" attesting that they were not communists and swearing fealty to the state and federal constitutions. Chapter 3 looks more closely at the effect loyalty oaths had on academic freedom and the imposition of official orthodoxy in other contexts. Here the concern relates to loyalty programs more broadly, including the appointment of governmental bodies tasked with exposing "disloyal" Americans, and their effects on expression and association.

Loyalty oaths compelled the expression of an official form of patriotism. Loyalty investigations, which were held at both the federal and states levels during the Second Red Scare, cast a repressive pall over *all* of the political opinions and affiliations of their subjects. Suspected disloyalty to the government cost many federal and state employees their reputations and their livelihoods.

When President Truman appointed the Temporary Committee on Employee Loyalty, he authorized a witch hunt in the federal service.[31] Thick FBI files were maintained on subjects, consisting of information about their political views and membership in "subversive" organizations. In the name of "national security," the federal government sought to ferret out subversives and other disloyal persons working in, or applying to work in, the federal service.

As Professor Stone notes, "During the Truman era (1947–53), more than 4.7 million individuals were investigated."[32] Although most were "cleared" of charges of disloyalty, the loyalty program discouraged individuals from serving in government, joining organizations that might be considered "subversive," and expressing dissenting opinions. President Eisenhower continued and even expanded the hunt for disloyal federal employees. When added together with the McCarthy and other anti-communism hearings, in terms of freedom of expression and association the costs of federal and state loyalty programs were extraordinary.

The First Amendment and Sedition

Wars end, domestic and global conditions shift, and the makeup of the Supreme Court changes. These and other circumstances contributed to the thawing of the Cold War, a reduction in public hysteria relating to communism and other foreign ideologies, and a broader interpretation of the First Amendment.

As did government officials and a majority of the American public, the Supreme Court gradually rejected the excesses and abuses of McCarthyism. It limited the application of the Smith Act and other means of prosecuting accused communists, socialists, and other radicals. In 1957, on what some have called "Red Monday," the Court handed down several decisions that favored accused communists.[33] Among other things, the Court reversed the Smith Act convictions of 14 individuals on the ground that they were based on mere advocacy of communism that did not present a "clear and present danger" of the violent overthrow of government.[34] The Court also invalidated state loyalty oath laws on First Amendment and other constitutional grounds.[35]

The Supreme Court's most direct reckoning with America's anti-sedition past came in *New York Times Co. v. Sullivan*, which was decided in 1964.[36] As discussed in chapter 1, the decision altered state libel laws, in particular as they related to defamation actions filed by public officials based on communications about their official conduct. The Court adopted the "actual malice" standard, which requires public official plaintiffs to prove that allegedly defamatory statements were made with knowledge of their falsity or reckless disregard for their truth.[37]

New York Times v. Sullivan also purported to settle the debate over the constitutionality of the Sedition Act of 1798.[38] The Court relied on the writings of Thomas Jefferson, James Madison, Justice Brandeis, and federal appeals court judge Learned Hand as evidence that prosecution of seditious libel would violate the First Amendment. It concluded that "although the Sedition Act was never tested in this Court, the attack upon its validity has carried the day in the court of history."[39] The justices noted that fines levied under the Act had been repaid, and that President Jefferson had pardoned speakers who had been convicted and sentenced. In doing so, Jefferson explained: "I discharged every person under punishment or prosecution under the sedition law because I considered, and now consider, that law to be a nullity, as absolute and as palpable as if Congress had ordered us to fall down and worship a golden image."[40] These historical events, the Court concluded, "reflect a broad consensus that the Act, because of the restraint it imposed upon criticism of government and public officials, was inconsistent with the [First Amendment]."[41]

Writing for the Court, Justice Brennan concluded that the nation's experience with the Sedition Act and with the offense of seditious libel more generally had "first crystallized a national awareness of the central meaning of the First Amendment."[42] That central meaning was based on the principle that debate on matters of public concern was supposed to be "uninhibited, robust, and wide-open." Thus, as discussed in chapter 1, the "central meaning" of the First Amendment is that Americans must be free, absent very narrow limitations, to discuss public matters and to criticize government—even in terms that "include vehement, caustic, and sometimes unpleasantly sharp attacks."[43]

The Court relied in part on a 1942 opinion by federal judge Henry White Edgerton, which he issued in a libel case filed by a congressman. Judge Edgerton wrote, "Cases which impose liability for erroneous reports of the political conduct of officials reflect the obsolete doctrine that the governed must not criticize their governors." He continued: "Political conduct and views which some respectable people approve, and others condemn, are constantly imputed to Congressmen. Errors of fact, particularly in regard to a man's mental states and processes, are inevitable. . . . Whatever is added to the field of libel is taken from the field of free debate."[44] As the Supreme Court observed, "criticism of official conduct does not lose its constitutional protection merely because it is effective criticism, and hence diminishes official reputations."[45]

New York Times Co. v. Sullivan sought to formally put an end to a long debate concerning the constitutionality of sedition prosecutions. It closed what Justice Douglas referred to as "one of our sorriest chapters." Among other things, the decision makes it exceedingly unlikely that governments will ever again enact laws providing directly for the punishment of communications and publications on the ground that they defame or are critical of government. Subsequent decisions extended First Amendment protection even to speech that advocated the overthrow of government, except in emergency circumstances where the government could prove that the threat was both likely to occur and imminent.[46]

Much earlier, in his concurring opinion in *Whitney v. California*, Justice Brandeis explained that suppression and censorship of speech critical of government violate central First Amendment principles of autonomy, self-government, and the search for truth. He wrote that the Founders "recognized the risks to which all human institutions are subject."[47] But, he explained, they "eschewed silence coerced by law—the argument of force in its worst form."[48] Brandeis observed that "order cannot be secured merely through fear of punishment for its infraction; that it is hazardous to discourage thought, hope and imagination; that fear breeds repression; that repression breeds hate; that hate menaces stable government; that the path of safety lies in the opportunity to discuss freely supposed grievances and proposed remedies; and that the fitting remedy for evil counsels is good ones."[49]

In terms of how the First Amendment is interpreted, the sedition experience highlighted the importance to a self-governing society of rights to think and speak openly—and critically—about government and government officials. The First Amendment's "central meaning" is central not only to how we view freedoms of press and speech, but more generally to our disposition toward the censorial power of government. The modern First Amendment incorporates Madison's understanding that the censorial power resides in the people and not in their government.

Sedition, Dissent, and the Democratic Experiment

We ought not to become complacent about the prospects for a return of the concept of seditious libel. Indeed, as discussed, the Trump Era has highlighted the danger of slipping into old habits. Even in times of relative world peace, domestic turmoil can create openings for authoritarian efforts to punish sedition and disloyalty. Those efforts may not take the form of criminal laws, but may have a similar impact on dissent. As we encounter new attacks on sedition during the Trump Era, it is critically important that we recall the lessons of history as they relate to punishment of seditious libel. In particular, we ought to pay close attention to how governments have sought to punish sedition even absent laws targeting it as such.

Americans have not faced sedition prosecutions—at least not by that name—for a century. However, governmental efforts to suppress criticism did not simply disappear when the nation's sedition laws were repealed. *New York Times Co. v. Sullivan* may have formally settled the First Amendment debate about the Sedition Act of 1798. However, the case did not put an end to official programs and actions designed to suppress dissident political activities or expression critical of the government or nation.

Like the concept of "sedition," measures designed to suppress criticism and dissent have taken a variety of forms. For instance, during the Vietnam

War era of the 1960s and 1970s, the federal government used law enforcement programs to expose and disrupt antiwar activism. It also went to court to restrain major newspapers from publishing the Pentagon Papers, a study critical of American involvement in the Vietnam War.[50] The federal government also sought to control or suppress various forms of political dissent—from burning draft cards, to disrespecting military uniforms, to defacing or burning the U.S. flag, to mass public protests.

The First Amendment was an effective rebuttal to some, but not all, of these efforts. The Supreme Court invalidated as a "prior restraint" the judicial injunction that ordered newspapers to cease publication of the Pentagon Papers, a decision that will play a substantial role in any future prosecution of Julian Assange and WikiLeaks.[51] It invalidated laws criminalizing the desecration of the flag.[52] But the First Amendment did not prevent surveillance of political dissidents, punishment for burning draft cards, or abusive public protest policing.[53]

Four general lessons emerge from the post-seditious libel experience. First, the danger of suppression is always with us—even in times of relative peace. Wars have long been associated with a special kind of public hysteria, which can have devastating and lasting effects on public dissent. However, as the Trump Era shows, we need to remain vigilant even in peacetime. From the Sedition Act to the present, only part of the rationale for suppressing dissent relates to its impact on the execution of war. Political retribution has also been a potent force motivating official efforts to stifle critics. Presidents have sought to stifle speakers who questioned the legitimacy of their elections—notably, a particular sore spot for the current president.

Second, punishment for sedition can take many different forms. The Trump administration has thus far relied upon vague threats to "investigate" critics and other norm-busting measures that skirt constitutional and legal lines. Revoking security clearances and making thinly veiled threats to use executive power to investigate search engines and satirical broadcasts are new. So, too, is the very public "war" on the press and the characterization of the press as "the enemy of the American people." The Trump administration likely is aware that it has even more direct and official powers at its disposal. For instance, in a declared national emergency, the Communications Act authorizes the president to take control of aspects of the communications infrastructure, including the internet. A president predisposed to censor his critics would not likely hesitate to exercise that authority.

Third, although the modern First Amendment can prevent some anti-sedition measures from being adopted or enforced, it will not protect political dissent from all forms of suppression. As discussed further in chapter 4, public protest restrictions are a good example. Similarly, revocation of security clearances may not violate the First Amendment—even if they are undertaken for retaliatory reasons. The president has wide discretion in terms of such revocations, and it is not clear that courts would enjoin him—particularly in the face of government arguments that revocation is necessary to national security. More generally, the First Amendment does not restrain the president or other officials from merely suggesting that critical commentary may result in some form of regulatory action. The president has a First Amendment right to criticize his critics. Up to a point, he may even threaten them with negative consequences.

Fourth, as the Cold War era acutely demonstrated, governmental attempts to suppress subversion and "disloyalty" create an adversary relationship between governments and their citizens. This relationship chills speech, press, and association. More broadly, it paralyzes democracy. As Madison observed in the Virginia Resolution, punishment for seditious speech "ought to produce universal alarm, because it is levelled against that right of freely examining public characters and measures, and of free communication among the people thereon, which has ever been justly deemed, the only effectual guardian of every other right." Measures that have recently been taken or threatened against ordinary citizens—including present and former government officials who choose to speak out, journalists, flag-burners, and technology companies—show the potential scope of this chilling effect.

During the Trump Era, hyper-partisanship, a presidential agenda that casts critics as disloyal enemies of the people, and a general societal intolerance for opposing viewpoints have created a toxic environment for political and cultural dissent. To be sure, the measures taken against dissidents have not been nearly as suppressive as in prior eras. However, some of the effects are quite familiar. As discussed further in chapter 3, this environment has once again led to calls for conformity, unity, and a brand of orthodox patriotism. Some of the president's supporters have complained that critics of the administration are acting seditiously or disloyally. This too echoes sentiments from America's repressive past.

As Professor Stone has documented, particularly during wartime, the speech of pacifists and radicals has been labeled seditious and disloyal.

Presidents from Adams to Nixon described negative media coverage, criticism of war, and the publication of government secrets as "seditious" or disloyal. After the terrorist attacks of September 11, 2001, antiwar protesters were sometimes characterized in the same manner.

As noted, what is partially unique about current calls for loyalty and complaints about "sedition" is that the United States is not formally at war with any foreign adversary. Declarations of war are not a condition precedent for attacks on civil liberties. We are at war with one another. Past eras have taught that governments can turn elements of society against one another. They have done so by falsely equating dissent with disloyalty. Through that false association, governments and entire societies have sought to create cultures of fear and conformity. They have denigrated protesters and intimidated the press.

Thus far, many administration critics and the press have generally stood their ground in the face of such attacks. In contrast to prior eras, when anti-communist hysteria deterred lawyers from representing dissidents, the legal profession has stepped forward to defend the rights of journalists and speakers. Unlike the passive silence of the Cold War era, some Americans have engaged in noisy acts of dissent.

Most Republicans, on the other hand, have been reluctant to criticize their party's leader—even in the face of sharp attacks on the press and dissenters. History teaches that this kind of complacency is dangerous. Suppression works in more than one partisan direction. The Tea Party and other conservative movements are just as much at risk from suppression of dissent as are today's left-leaning movements. If future presidents wage open warfare on the press and dissidents , the culture of dissent will be placed at risk.

There is an appetite, as shown by public polling numbers relating to questions about presidential control of the media, for suppressing negative, critical, or "fake" news coverage. The president's supporters have also raised no objections when he has suggested jailing or denaturalizing dissident speakers. They reject any insinuation that the president's rhetoric might have contributed to physical threats and attacks on his critics—even when the attackers parrot the president's own criticisms of those who have been threatened or attacked.

Democracy may survive under these conditions, but it will not thrive or reach its full potential. As Americans have learned, democracy depends not on loyalty to a party or an individual personality, but rather to certain fundamental principles. Among these principles is the notion that criticism of government benefits the political community by informing the public, exposing corruption, and resisting would-be autocrats.

A government's responsiveness to criticism and dissent speaks to both the robustness of the democracy it governs and its own legitimacy. In autocracies, dissent is not tolerated. In democracies, speaking truth to power is essential to self-government. Presidents who target criticism and proclaim it to be seditious, subversive, or disloyal preside over weaker and less legitimate democracies than do those who tolerate dissent and protect civil liberties.

At the time of this writing, we are now just one year past the first Sedition Act's centenary. This is an appropriate time to revisit Justice Holmes's now-famous dissent in *Abrams v. United States*. A majority of the Court upheld the convictions of political pamphleteers under the Espionage Act and Sedition Act. However, as Justice Holmes observed, "Persecution for the expression of opinions seems to me perfectly logical. If you have no doubt of your premises or your power and want a certain result with all your heart you naturally express your wishes in law and sweep away all opposition."[54] Looking back on the lessons of America's first Sedition Act, Holmes argued that the First Amendment prohibits governments from suppressing their critics.

As Professor Stone observed in his study of dissent in times of war, "It is, of course, much easier to look back on past crises and find our predecessors wanting than to make wise judgments when we ourselves are in the eye of the storm. But that challenge now falls to this generation of Americans."[55] The democratic experiment depends on internalizing the First Amendment lessons of our forebears, who did not always resist hysteria and conformity, but who charted a path forward toward freedom in the face of fear.

3

The Anti-orthodoxy Principle

If there is any fixed star in our constitutional constellation, it is that no official, high or petty, can prescribe what shall be orthodox in politics, nationalism, religion, or other matters of opinion or force citizens to confess by word or act their faith therein.[1]

Governments communicate in order to execute policies and influence public opinion. They speak their institutional and official minds, and convey viewpoints with regard to a broad range of matters of public concern. The president and other government officials are permitted to weigh in on the social and political controversies of the day, and their opinions can add significant information to the marketplace of ideas relating to such matters.

Although they are generally free to speak their minds, governments cannot coerce others to adopt or convey their official positions. Thus, they may not compel or command individuals to communicate viewpoints the government favors but the speakers do not personally hold. Nor can governments punish individuals for expressing viewpoints that differ from the party line.

One important implication of the distinction between speaking and regulating is that with regard to politics, religion, patriotism, and other matters, governments cannot insist on the adoption or expression of any official orthodoxy. They cannot force us to believe what is not in our hearts, or put words in our mouths. This "anti-orthodoxy principle" is a central pillar of the First Amendment. It protects speakers' autonomy interests and their right to dissent. It also facilitates self-government and the search for truth by protecting speakers from official coercion with regard to ideas, opinions, and beliefs.

As we will see, the anti-orthodoxy principle has been a critically important feature of the First Amendment tradition. It is a product of the historical repudiation of coercive measures, including laws mandating flag

The First Amendment in the Trump Era. Timothy Zick.
© Timothy Zick 2019. Published 2019 by Oxford University Press.

salutes, protecting the American flag and other symbols of nationhood from desecration and disrespect, and requiring the execution of "loyalty oaths." The anti-orthodoxy principle has protected political, religious, and other forms of public and private dissent. As with new regulations of "sedition," discussed in chapter 2, the Trump Era has raised new concerns about efforts to coerce orthodoxy. These concerns have centered around conflicts involving flag-burning, the National Anthem, and the Pledge of Allegiance, but are part of a broader agenda to instill official orthodoxy.

Flag, Fealty, and Faith

President Trump has frequently expressed his personal views concerning matters pertaining to issues such as patriotism, religion, and "loyalty." As noted, he is entitled to communicate these views. But the president has also made statements suggestive of a more coercive agenda that conflicts with the anti-orthodoxy principle.

The Trump Era has once again placed "nationalism" front and center in our political discourse. The president's "America First" agenda is presumably a manifestation of his personal and official views concerning patriotism and loyalty to government and country. Like his predecessors, President Trump has praised members of the armed forces, first responders, and immigration enforcement officers. At public rallies and on social media, the president has frequently proclaimed his "love" for the United States. He has also criticized and demonized immigrants, refugees, and Islam—all, not coincidentally, persons or faiths associated with foreign nations.[2]

As a candidate and later as president, Trump has also expressed the view that people should more frequently, vocally, and publicly recognize and praise God. He has made a point of saying that Americans should say "Merry Christmas" to one another during the holidays (apparently in the mistaken belief that this is not already routinely done). Indeed, he has insisted that they are actually *doing so* to a greater extent during his presidency than during his predecessor's. The president has also focused special attention on the words "under God" in the Pledge of Allegiance. In public appearances and on social media, he has opined that those words deserve special emphasis.

Again, the First Amendment does not prohibit the president from holding or communicating these views.[3] Governments and public officials have long expressed similar sentiments. Presidents, in particular, often express strong feelings about matters of patriotism and faith. Governments express these sentiments in a variety of different ways—by honoring veterans and active duty military personnel, marking religious holidays, and celebrating patriotism and nationalism. However, as discussed in more detail later in this chapter, the First Amendment prohibits presidents and other officials from taking a more coercive approach to nationalism and other subjects.

Thus, for example, President Trump has suggested that individuals who burn the U.S. flag should be jailed and stripped of their citizenship. That would plainly amount to imposing sanctions for making a political statement at odds with the government's own views about the flag. Under current First Amendment precedents, this would be patently unconstitutional.

President Trump has also suggested that National Football League players who have taken a knee during the playing of the National Anthem and the display of the U.S. flag should be punished for doing so. As the players have explained, they are not protesting the flag, the nation, or the U.S. military.[4] Rather, they are seeking to draw attention to social justice issues, including what they view as a form of police brutality—in particular, incidents in which police officers have shot and killed unarmed African Americans.[5]

By contrast, President Trump has consistently characterized these protests as unpatriotic and disloyal. He has criticized athletes for being ungrateful, apparently owing to the financial and other successes they have enjoyed by virtue of their talents. The president has argued that the protests demonstrate "disrespect" for the National Anthem, the flag, and the nation's military.[6] He has publicly branded those who disagree as disloyal and unpatriotic.

In this dispute, the president has come close to crossing, if he has not in fact stepped over, the First Amendment line separating expression of his views on the matter from unlawful official coercion. He has suggested that players should be fired for participating in these political protests. During a public rally, he suggested that team owners should respond to the protests by saying, "Get that son of a bitch off the field right now. Out! He's fired. He's fired!" The next day, President Trump tweeted that the players should stand for the anthem or "YOURE FIRED. Find something else to do!" In comments directed to NFL owners, he said that they "should change their policy" allowing the protests, that they "must respect" his view that the protests were offensive, and that they should "fire or suspend" the kneeling players. He also called for a public boycott of NFL games, at least until the protesting players were fired or suspended. Several months later, the NFL announced a new policy of fining teams if their players kneeled during the anthem.

President Trump has not made the same coercive overtures regarding religious expression. But he has implied that America will be "great again" only when its people greet each other in a certain manner during the holidays and stop questioning the inclusion of references to God in the National Anthem. As discussed in chapter 2, he has insisted on "loyalty"—primarily to himself, as interactions with various aides suggest, but also to a certain vision of America.

During the Trump Era, several conditions have contributed to renewed pressure to conform to the government's views on matters such as patriotism and faith. It is a renewal because, as we will see, prior governments and officials have similarly insisted—some even more directly than the current president—that citizens adopt and express particular orthodoxies.

As noted, the president was elected based on an "America First" political and policy agenda. That agenda trades heavily on nationalism, ideas about appropriate displays of patriotism, and the invasion of foreign persons and religions. Flags and faith are effective unifying forces, particularly for political bases. Without a war to rally around, such symbols can be relied upon as alterative means for stirring up nationalistic sentiments.

Indeed, even the apparently religious agenda described earlier may actually be based on a form of nationalism. President Trump has vocally courted and strongly identified with evangelical voters. A recent study suggests that religious groups are not the primary target audience for the "Merry Christmas" and "under God" parts of the Trump orthodoxy agenda.[7] Rather, the study concludes that the president's focus on faith is actually part of the same nationalism agenda that is associated with the slogan "make American great again." In other words, the president's supporters are embracing "Merry Christmas" and "under God" not out of some deeply held religious views, but rather owing to their political conservatism. In particular, white political conservatives have embraced this aspect of official orthodoxy owing to their political and cultural insecurities. Thus, in the Trump Era, the "War on Christmas" is less about Christianity than it is about a form of cultural or political dominance.

The general political climate has also contributed to the revival of this agenda. The notion that those with whom one disagrees ought to be "locked up" hearkens back to periods when dissenters were jailed and treated as "un-American" traitors. Those who prefer "Happy Holidays" to "Merry Christmas," or who object to references to God as part of a national creed, are viewed as aligned not just against Christianity or faith but also the United States.

Not for the first time (think Muhammad Ali, for example), the world of sport is bound up with politics and partisanship. Similarly, the "War on Christmas" has been an aspect of our culture wars for decades.

However, the Trump Era seems to have brought a new edge and urgency to these matters. Opinion polling suggests that many Americans support President Trump's position that kneeling during the anthem is disrespectful and unpatriotic.[8] NFL fans threatened to boycott the league over the player protests. In Indiana, a state legislator proposed a law that would have entitled fans to a refund if they attended a game at which players silently protested during the National Anthem. And when Nike made Colin Kaepernick, who initiated the NFL protests, the face of its most recent marketing initiative videos appeared on social media showing owners of Nike sneakers burning the shoes (sometimes while still wearing them!) in protest.

Faith has also been weaponized as a partisan wedge issue—again, not for the first time, but in ways that are unique to the Trump Era. Even seemingly petty matters such as what counts as a proper season's greeting cause conflict and consternation. Religious adherents believe they are under siege and marginalized in the political community, while those who urge separation of church and state likewise feel their principles are under attack. Like politicians before him, President Trump has positioned himself to take political advantage of these divisions. Indeed, he has exploited and exacerbated them.

As noted in the Introduction, my primary concern is not whether the president's statements or proposals would actually violate the First Amendment or whether the president could be haled into court as a result of them. The broader concern relates to how governments contribute to an environment in which matters such as patriotism and faith become grounds for division or polarization rather than subjects of serious public debate or even national unity.

Whether the president or the government is using the coercive power of law to force individuals to salute the flag or give voice to particular scripts regarding the flag or faith, the specter of orthodoxy persists. That does not mean we should ignore the tangible and intangible consequences of the orthodoxy agenda. It is no small thing for the president of the United States to publicly advocate that political dissidents be jailed and denaturalized. That the "leader of the free world" would publicly advocate that position ought to alarm freedom- and flag-loving Americans of all political persuasions. In the Trump Era, such statements tend to be buried in the avalanche of news that counts as a "news cycle" or laughed off, much like the president's public musings about Christmas greetings. These are serious matters, and they deserve serious attention.

Even if they are not jailed or arrested, demonizing flag-burners may lead to their arrest for other offenses or to vigilante violence. Flag-burning is an unpopular form of dissent, and branding it "un-American" or even treasonous will have ramifications for those who engage in it—whether or not any law on the books prohibits the flag's desecration. The orthodoxy agenda may also lead to the revival of proposals to amend the Constitution to ban flag-burning—something Congress has considered and rejected on a number of occasions. Similarly, religious adherents, agnostics, and atheists will all be affected personally and culturally by an orthodoxy agenda that effectively chooses sides with regard to matters of faith.

The chapter aims to meet head-on the core arguments made on behalf of the Trump orthodoxy agenda. One argument is that burning the flag or silently taking a knee during the National Anthem are singularly unpatriotic acts that ought to be punished. Underlying that sentiment is the conviction that there is one (and only one) appropriate response to the flag or the playing of the anthem—standing at attention, hand over heart, singing the National Anthem. Similarly, the notion that all ought to mouth the same holiday greetings is based on the sentiment that there is one (and only one) appropriate message to send during that particular time of the year. These arguments go to the heart of, and indeed offend, the First Amendment's anti-orthodoxy principle.

The Constitution's "Fixed Star"

Despite the unique forms they have taken during the Trump Era, efforts to compel patriotic and nationalistic displays are not a new phenomenon. As discussed in chapter 2, governmental agendas to compel unity and punish dissent have been distressingly common, particularly during wartime. State and national governments have sought to compel patriotic displays in the interest of national unity and national security.

In 1943, the Supreme Court dealt a fatal blow to laws seeking to impose an official orthodoxy regarding the U.S. flag. In *West Virginia State Board of Education v. Barnette*,[9] the Supreme Court invalidated state laws mandating that public school children salute the U.S. flag and recite the Pledge of Allegiance as part of a daily school ritual. *Barnette* was the first precedent to articulate the anti-orthodoxy principle. The decision is generally viewed as being among the most important First Amendment decisions the Supreme Court has ever handed down.

Three years earlier, in 1940, *Minersville School District v. Gobitis* had upheld the same compulsory flag exercises. Writing for the Court in *Gobitis*, Justice Frankfurter, over a single dissent, rejected the claims of Jehovah's Witnesses that the compulsory flag salute and pledge violated their First Amendment free exercise of religion and free speech rights. The Court pointed to "national unity," which it claimed was closely associated with "national security," as state interests of the highest order. After *Gobitis*, many Jehovah's Witnesses were treated as suspected traitors and Nazi sympathizers. Outbreaks of vigilante violence against Jehovah's Witnesses were common.

In *Barnette*, the Court sharply reversed course. It invalidated a West Virginia law that compelled public school children to stand and salute the U.S. flag during the recitation of the Pledge of Allegiance at the beginning of each school day. Justice Jackson, writing for the Court, stated, "To sustain the compulsory flag salute we are required to say that a Bill of Rights which guards the individual's right to speak his own mind, left it open to public authorities to compel him to utter what is not in his mind." While the Court acknowledged that the state could foster and promote national unity through persuasion and example, it held that governments could not achieve those same ends through mandates and compulsion.

In response to West Virginia's argument that its interest in "national unity" overrode the students' right not to be compelled to communicate the state's message, the Court responded that "[s]truggles to coerce uniformity of sentiment in support of some end thought essential to their time and country have been waged by many good as well as by evil men."[10] It continued, "Those who begin coercive elimination of dissent soon find themselves exterminating dissenters. Compulsory unification of opinion achieves only the unanimity of the graveyard."[11] The Court concluded that insisting on a particular response to the National Anthem and the U.S. flag "invades the sphere of intellect and spirit which it is the purpose of the First Amendment to our Constitution to reserve from all official control."[12]

The Court also responded to the argument that government is empowered to mandate patriotic observances, particularly during times of war. To this claim it responded, "To believe that patriotism will not flourish if patriotic ceremonies are voluntary and spontaneous instead of a compulsory routine is to make an unflattering estimate of the appeal of our institutions to free minds." Justice Jackson punctuated his iconic opinion with the quotation from the beginning of this chapter, "*If there is any fixed star in our constitutional constellation, it is that no official, high or petty, can prescribe what shall be orthodox in politics, nationalism, religion, or other matters of opinion or force citizens to confess by word or act their faith therein.*"[13]

"No official—high or petty." *Barnette* stands for the proposition that government officials at all levels are prohibited from compelling individuals to communicate viewpoints they do not hold or support. It bars the government from compelling private speakers to support or espouse official orthodoxy in politics, faith, and other matters.

This anti-orthodoxy principle has been invoked by a wide variety of dissenters in response to official compulsion. For example, the Supreme Court held that a Jehovah's Witness could not be compelled by the State of New Hampshire to convey the state motto, "Live Free or Die," on his car's license plate.[14] Like the children and their parents in *Barnette*, the driver objected that the motto compelled expression of a view that conflicted with his religious beliefs. The organizer of an Irish-American pride parade in Boston also invoked the anti-orthodoxy principle, to invalidate a state command that he include an LGBT group in the parade.[15]

Recent decisions have similarly invoked and enforced *Barnette*'s anti-orthodoxy principle. In one case, the Supreme Court invalidated state laws compelling public employees to pay union dues, on the ground that the laws compelled political speech by dues-paying members.[16] In another, the Court invalidated state laws mandating that crisis pregnancy centers, which object to abortion and do not provide abortion services, communicate messages regarding abortion services to their patients.[17] The right not to be compelled to speak has also shielded political activists from government requirements that they disclose their identities.[18] It has prohibited government from compelling private property owners to allow outside speakers to use those properties to communicate messages the owners reject.[19]

Critics contend that in some of these decisions, the Court misapplied the so-called "compelled speech" doctrine. My point is not that all of the decisions are correct on their merits. Rather, I mention them to demonstrate the importance and potential scope of the anti-orthodoxy principle. As these decisions illustrate, from a First Amendment perspective two separate aspects of speech compulsion are problematic. The first concern is that the mandates interfere with speaker autonomy. Mandatory pledges and the like compel speakers to communicate against their will. The second concern with speech mandates is that they empower government to use private speakers to broadcast and establish an "approved" set of beliefs regarding national unity, politics, abortion, sexual orientation, and other matters. Those official orthodoxies are then attributed to the speakers, in a manner that falsely suggests support for them.

Both concerns are present in the context of laws restricting certain offensive displays relating to the U.S. flag or other official symbols. The flag is a highly communicative symbol. For many Americans, it represents ideas relating to patriotism, military service, and national unity. But for many others, it does not speak to those ideals at all—indeed, it may communicate messages that conflict with religious and other beliefs. Compelling the communication of respect for the flag forces individuals to espouse beliefs they do not hold and establishes official orthodoxy through compulsion.

Just as government cannot compel others to communicate its views with respect to the flag and patriotism, it cannot punish those who communicate sentiments contrary to those the government prefers. Thus, the Supreme Court has invalidated laws that purport to compel respect for the flag. In *Texas v. Johnson*,[20] the Court invalidated a Texas law that banned any person from intentionally "*desecrating*" the U.S. flag. The law defined "desecration" as any act "defacing, damaging, or otherwise physically mistreating" the flag "in a way that the actor knows will seriously offend one or more persons likely to observe or discover" the act. Johnson, who was attending a political protest in Dallas, burned an American flag as nearby protesters shouted, "America, the red, white, and blue, we spit on you." No one was physically injured by the flag-burning, although some indicated that they were offended by what Johnson had done.

The Supreme Court rejected Texas's argument that it had an overriding interest in "preserving the flag as a symbol of nationhood and national unity." As the Court observed, Johnson was "prosecuted for his expression of dissatisfaction with the policies of this country, expression situated at the core of our First Amendment values." However, a "bedrock principle underlying the First Amendment . . . is that the Government may not prohibit the expression of an idea simply because society finds the idea itself offensive or disagreeable."[21] Invoking *Barnette's* iconic passage, the Court wrote, "We would be permitting a State to 'prescribe what shall be orthodox' by saying that one may burn the flag to convey one's attitude toward it and its referents only if one does not endanger the flag's representation of nationhood and national unity."[22] The Court also noted, "We never before have held that the Government may ensure that a symbol be used to express only one view of that symbol or its referents."[23]

Thus, with regard to the U.S. flag, the Court declined to create an exception to what it referred to as the "joust of principles protected by the First Amendment."[24] Thus, it observed, "the way to preserve the flag's special role is not to punish those who feel differently about these matters. It is to persuade them that they are wrong."[25] The justices could "imagine no more appropriate response to a burning flag than waving one's own, no better way to counter a flag-burner's message than by saluting the flag that burns, no surer means of preserving the dignity even of the flag that burned than by . . . according its remains a respectful burial."[26]

Barnette and *Johnson* rest on bedrock First Amendment principles and values. However, as President Trump's public comments and proposals suggest, not everyone is convinced of their application in the context of flag-burning. In his dissent in *Johnson*, Chief Justice Rehnquist wrote that he could find little worth protecting insofar as flag-burning is concerned. He referred to the act as an "inarticulate grunt or roar" that added little or nothing of consequence to social or political discourse.[27] Many Americans apparently agree. Opinion polling shows that a majority of Americans have supported amending the Constitution to outlaw flag-burning.[28] Although Congress has considered such amendments on several occasions, thus far legislative support has fallen short of the mark needed to propose ratification of a constitutional amendment by the states. In response to *Johnson*, Congress did enact a federal law, similar to the Texas defacement statute, which criminalized disrespectful treatment of the flag. The Supreme Court invalidated that law too, for essentially the same reasons it had provided in *Johnson*.[29]

As noted, the anti-orthodoxy principle continues to be a core aspect of the First Amendment's protection for speaker autonomy and the right to dissent. Under existing precedents, jailing or denaturalizing someone for burning the flag as a symbolic act of political protest, as President Trump has suggested, is a nonstarter. Governmental pressure to conform to officially approved beliefs, viewpoints, or sentiments concerning patriotism and faith creates an environment in which dissenting views may be chilled or suppressed. The government may express opinions concerning these and other matters, but its use of coercive powers violates the anti-orthodoxy principle.

A "Pall of Orthodoxy"

Chapter 2's discussion of "sedition" observed that governments have sometimes sought to compel "loyalty" to the United States—including from government officials and employees. It focused in particular on the First Amendment concerns raised by the false equation of dissent and disloyalty. The chapter also briefly discussed the demands for various types of loyalty—to nation, administration, and president—that have been prevalent during the Trump Era. As *Barnette* and its progeny suggest, efforts to compel national loyalty also implicate the anti-orthodoxy principle that is the focus of this chapter.

Not all oaths are pernicious or unconstitutional. For example, the Constitution requires presidents to take an oath to preserve and protect the Constitution.[30] Members of Congress, federal judges, and state officers also take a similar oath of office.[31] As public officers, these individuals have special duties and obligations connected with their service in government. Resident aliens have also long been required to take an oath of loyalty to the United States as a condition of their naturalization. This oath, which is ceremonial in nature, is a means of formalizing a person's citizenship status.

The *coercive* use of loyalty oaths and pledges, on the other hand, raises serious First Amendment anti-orthodoxy concerns. As discussed in chapter 2, loyalty oaths were used during the Cold War to regulate and suppress dissent.[32] In 1947, President Harry S. Truman instituted a Loyalty Program when he signed Executive Order 9835, "Prescribing Procedures for the Administration of an Employees Loyalty Program in the Executive Branch of the Government." The Order required employees to sign loyalty oaths and called for investigations to root out "disloyal or subversive" government employees to ensure "unswerving loyalty to the United States government." Under this program, "loyalty" was used as a condition of federal employment.

During the Cold War, national and state governments similarly demanded that employees, teachers, public aid recipients, and others sign

loyalty oaths expressing their support for the United States and/or particular states. In addition, as a condition of employment or benefits, these
individuals were required to deny membership in communist or other
"subversive" organizations.

Loyalty oaths were particularly controversial on public university
campuses. During the Cold War period, faculty members at the University
of California were required, by state law, to sign oaths affirming their loyalty
to the California state constitution and denying membership or belief in organizations, including communist organizations, advocating the overthrow
of the U.S. government. In the summer of 1950, 31 non-signers, including
some prominent Jewish scholars who had survived the Holocaust, were
dismissed from employment. Public housing residents and students receiving financial aid also became targets of loyalty programs. This angered
one U.S. senator from Massachusetts, John F. Kennedy, who wrote, "The
loyalty oath has no place in a program designed to encourage education. It
is distasteful, humiliating."

Although it had articulated the anti-orthodoxy principle in *Barnette*, the
Supreme Court did not initially rule that these loyalty oath mandates were
unconstitutional. Prior to the 1960s, there was little protection for radical
speech, including speech supporting communism or revolution (peaceful
or otherwise). The First Amendment did not yet protect a right of "association" that would protect joining political parties, including "subversive"
organizations.

During the 1960s, the Supreme Court invalidated state loyalty oaths on
First Amendment and other constitutional grounds. In 1964, the Court held
that two Washington statutes that required public school teachers to "promote respect for the flag and the institutions of the United States of America
and the State of Washington" and affirm that they were not "subversive" and
not aiding the Communist Party of the United States were too vague to be
enforced.[33] The Court also invalidated a 1961 Arizona statute that required
current and potential state employees to sign a loyalty oath, on the ground
that it violated the freedom of political association guaranteed by the First
Amendment.[34]

On university campuses, loyalty oaths collided sharply with principles
of academic freedom. The Supreme Court recognized this special concern
when it declared unconstitutional a New York State law that banned the
hiring or retention of "subversives" in teaching and other public employee
jobs.[35] An English instructor at the State University of New York at Buffalo

refused to sign an oath stating that he was not a communist. As a result, his contract was not renewed.

The Court ruled that the New York law and regulations violated the First Amendment. It found special cause for concern in the effect such laws would likely have on academic freedom on campuses. The Court observed, "Our nation is deeply committed to safeguarding academic freedom, which is of transcendent value to all of us and not merely to the teachers concerned. That freedom is therefore a special concern of the First Amendment, which does not tolerate laws that cast *a pall of orthodoxy* over the classroom."[36]

These precedents did not eliminate all forms of loyalty oath requirements from federal or state laws. Today, many federal civil service employees are still asked to sign them. State employees, including faculty members at some universities, are also asked to sign loyalty oaths as a condition of hiring or retention. These oaths, stripped of the "anti-radicalism" language the Supreme Court found offensive in the 1960s cases, generally require that the employee pledge loyalty to federal and state constitutions and promise to protect these from enemies both foreign and domestic. In this form, they are similar to the constitutional oaths taken by the president and other constitutional officers.

Even in this form, not all government employees are willing to sign loyalty oaths. For example, in 2015, James Sallis, an adjunct writing instructor at Phoenix College, refused to sign a loyalty oath that would have attested that he "bore true faith and allegiance to" the U.S. and Arizona constitutions. When told that signing the oath was a condition of his retention and that he would not be granted an exemption, Sallis resigned his position. In contrast, most employees subject to loyalty oaths sign them. Some may find them unobjectionable. Others may consider signing the oath an expression of commitment to service or their own individual patriotism. Many more may simply view the exercise as meaningless—a bureaucratic detail, or a pledge that does not carry any specific burdens, duties, or penalties.

Loyalty oaths are used to assure fealty to different causes and sentiments. As the Supreme Court ultimately recognized, when they are used as a condition of receiving some public benefit oaths can be unconstitutionally coercive. In that context, they can be used to extract a sentiment or ideology that the speaker does not believe in or wish to express. In that sense, they are similar to the mandate struck down in *Barnette* and laws that criminalize the "defacement" of the U.S. flag.

As the Supreme Court has observed, loyalty oaths can "cast a pall of orthodoxy" over classrooms. Mandatory oaths are particularly troublesome in the context of the classroom, where compelled orthodoxy threatens the free exchange of ideas. Unlike presidents and legislators, university professors and other educators do not perform the functions of constitutional officers. They operate in the world of ideas. Some of these ideas may be critical or dismissive of constitutional principles, understandings, or underpinnings. In that context, in particular, the loyalty oath poses significant threats to the marketplace of ideas and the expression of dissent. But mandatory oaths can also create similar problems in government workplaces and agencies. Demanding, rather than inspiring, loyalty to a cause or program may suppress criticism of government and result in false perceptions of acceptance or "loyalty."

Orthodoxy and Dissent

As *Barnette, Johnson*, and the loyalty oath cases demonstrate, government cannot dictate national unity, compel expression of state-approved patriotic messages, or insist that individuals advocate or hold only approved theories of government. The First Amendment's anti-orthodoxy principle prohibits these forms of compulsion. However, governments can express strong views about patriotism and faith, and indeed can exert some pressure on the public to adopt their points of view. In this context, then, it is important to mark some distinctions between official compulsion and official expression.

As noted, President Trump's proposal that flag-burners be jailed or denaturalized is a direct form of regulation. One would hope that it will never be adopted as law, and if it is that the courts will resoundingly reject its premise. Absent a constitutional amendment, flag-burning and other forms of "desecration" will likely remain a protected form of political speech.

Loyalty oaths, at least of the kind enforced during the Cold War era, are also likely a relic of the past. At least to this point, the president has not ordered executive branch officials to sign loyalty oaths or statements disclaiming membership in "radical" or "subversive" groups as a condition of employment (although he has reportedly required some executive branch appointees to sign nondisclosure agreements). Nor has he proposed any law or regulation that requires citizens to greet one another with

"Merry Christmas." or some other mandated script. These kinds of actions would also clearly violate not just the First Amendment's anti-orthodoxy free speech principle, as well as its prohibition on the "establishment" of religion.

But what about less direct or subtler measures? The president's intervention in the NFL protests offers an example of the constitutional lines we need to be concerned about. The NFL is a private organization. As such, it is not required to abide by the First Amendment—only "state actors" such as governments or public officials must do so. Thus, when commentators speak about the players' "free speech rights" vis-à-vis their *employer*, they are technically off base.

However, government officials and regulators are subject to the First Amendment's commands. Some of President Trump's statements approach the line of speech compulsion implicated in cases such as *Barnette*. For example, his suggestion that the NFL could lose its antitrust exemption or its "massive tax breaks" if the league did not punish players for protesting points toward the sort of regulatory measures that trigger the First Amendment.[37] This is similar to the line the president has approached when promising to "look into" or "investigate" broadcast licenses, Google's algorithm, and *Saturday Night Live's* parody sketches.

As with many of the president's public statements, it has been difficult to discern his intent with regard to the NFL players and owners. Short of actually regulating these individuals or their organizations in some manner, most of the president's statements likely amount to government or even private speech permitted by the First Amendment.

As noted, the president is entitled to express his own views regarding the NFL and its players, both as an official and as a private citizen. Similarly, he may express his views on the "proper" way to celebrate the holidays and his support for reference to God in the Pledge of Allegiance. Absent compulsion, punishment, or retaliation, official orthodoxy agendas do not run afoul of the First Amendment.

However, that does not mean we ought to welcome these statements, or treat them as wholly unrelated to the anti-orthodoxy principle. To the contrary, a "pall of orthodoxy" can arise in an environment in which individuals do not view themselves as free to dissent from orthodox views. Whether or not the president has violated the First Amendment, his communications create pressure to conform and thereby corrode speaker autonomy.

When the president of the United States refers to protesting NFL players as "weak and out of control," says "son of a bitch" players should be fired, and characterizes their protests as "disrespecting our country," his sentiments carry the significant weight of the office he occupies. They encourage political supporters and the public at large to treat even peaceful displays of dissent as evidence that the dissenter is unpatriotic and disloyal.

As discussed further in chapter 5's examination of "hate speech," as speaker government can be a positive influence on the nation's public discourse. It can encourage values such as equality, self-government, and tolerance.[38] These are precisely the values at play in the debate over the NFL protests, which originated from concerns about equality and social justice. In similar ways, government speech about faith and religion can also facilitate public discourse. It can encourage pluralism and tolerance rather than preference and division.

The point is not that the government must or should remain silent about important matters such as patriotism and faith—it should not be. Nor, of course, is any government official required to agree with or adopt the cause of those who disagree with its viewpoints. However, government speakers can use their platforms in ways that encourage open dialog about matters of public concern and tolerance for those who dissent from the preferred views of majorities or vocal pluralities. Government officials can do these things while at the same time expressing support for the military, law enforcement, and national unity.

By contrast, when governments throw their weight behind political or cultural orthodoxies, they play a very different and much more negative role. As history shows, orthodoxy agendas divide the public and fundamentally change its relationship with government. Protest and dissent become marginalized. Dissenters are treated as disloyal and "un-American." Further, insisting on conformity with an official orthodoxy teaches the public that the appropriate response to speech we dislike is to insist that it be brought into conformity with majority or vocal minority viewpoints.

The principal lesson of the anti-orthodoxy principle is that there is no single appropriate way to react to the National Anthem, the flag, the nation, or the holiday season. Freedom of speech means that individuals get to decide how to react to such things, and what meaning to ascribe to them. There is a diversity of views with regard to what it means to be loyal to one's country or faithful to one's religion. The anti-orthodoxy principle rejects the insistence that all must kneel, stand, bow, sing, or otherwise conduct themselves in the same manner.

Another core First Amendment principle, related to the anti-orthodoxy principle, is that the remedy for speech we dislike is counter-speech and not enforced uniformity.[39] Thus, NFL fans can criticize the players and the owners, and can decline to attend games. Apparel owners can burn their shoes in protest (although they ought to take them off first). Those offended by the players' protests, including the president, can stand at reverent attention as a means of expressing the view that they think the players are wrong or misguided. As the Supreme Court suggested in *Johnson*, people can respond to flag-burning by saluting the flag. Christians who feel marginalized can greet everyone with "Merry Christmas!," and others can extend an equally heartfelt "Happy Holidays" in return.

The First Amendment's preference for counter-speech over coercive regulation is based on the notion that society benefits when opposing views meet in the marketplace of ideas and compete for public acceptance. For this plan to work, however, dissent must at least be tolerated and ideally embraced. Sadly, that has not been the case in recent public debates about patriotism, faith, and other matters. Increasingly, it seems that disagreement of any kind is seen as unwelcome, unfriendly, or even threatening.

Consider again the case of the NFL protesters, whose conduct and expression has been neither violent nor disruptive. No one has been prevented from seeing, hearing, or participating in the pregame ceremonies. Nor have the protests affected the game itself. Indeed, the protests have been model examples of peaceful and nonviolent dissent. That means that the objection and desire for retribution cannot stem from disruption or interference with the rights of others. The protesters are not blocking traffic, blasting their message into someone's home, or otherwise disturbing the public peace.

And yet, according to some, these protests have "ruined the game." The nature of the objection necessarily must go to the *content* of these symbolic protests. However, there is at the same time an almost willful refusal to hear what the protesters are actually saying—an ironic affirmation of their social justice critique.

The president's characterization of the players on Twitter as individuals "showing total disrespect to our Flag & Country" misrepresents both the intent and substance of their message. Describing them as protests *against* the flag, the military, or the country is false and divisive. This "official" interpretation divides the public by stoking disapproval and anger rather than counseling tolerance and understanding. It disrupts the "marketplace of ideas"—first by misstating the message, and then by encouraging its suppression.

The NFL protests raise a broad concern of the book—namely how, particularly in a hyper-partisan era, Americans can resist the desire to dismiss or censor viewpoints concerning nationalism, religion, equality, and other matters. We live in an era in which tolerance for dissenting viewpoints is starting to dip to the historic lows we experienced during the Cold War, when public hysteria produced suspicion and fear of "subversive" persons and ideas. As tolerance dissipates, calls for orthodoxy tend to increase.

This general concern taps into current debates about "political correctness." Conservatives complain that liberals want to suppress speech they disagree with, and some indeed have taken that wrongheaded position. But orthodoxy works both ways. The same person complaining of the "snowflake" liberal who cannot tolerate conservative ideas would gladly suppress speech she views as unpatriotic or disrespectful of the flag or the military. Indeed, during prior eras, conservative orthodoxy drove the hunt for "subversives" and "radicals." In the present era, "both sides" are more comfortable hearing and seeing messages that are consistent with their own beliefs.

Today most Americans would presumably reject government efforts to lock up individuals solely for studying socialism or praising dictators. However, certain forms of dissent, such as flag-burning, kneeling during the National Anthem, or "Happy Holidays" still seem to trigger a strong public backlash.

The political philosopher John Stuart Mill, whose work significantly influenced the Founders' conception of free speech and press, wrote disapprovingly of the "tyranny of the majority." He observed that although official censorship and compulsion are dangerous, society itself could act like a tyrant. Thus, Mill wrote, "[p]rotection . . . against the tyranny of the magistrate is not enough; there needs protection also against the tendency of society to impose, by means other than civil penalties, its own ideas and practices as rules of conduct on those who dissent from them."[40] We might add to Mill's concern the prospect of a "tyranny of the minority"— particularly a minority stoked and backed by the most powerful office in the land.

Characterizing dissenters as unpatriotic or indicating that certain holiday greeters may be un-Christian or even un-American highlights the dangers Mill warned about. The First Amendment's anti-orthodoxy principle counteracts cultural impulses to suppress dissent. It rests on the understanding that patriotism cannot be legislated or otherwise compelled, but must be the product of well-informed and ultimately voluntary choices. The anti-orthodoxy principle is not partisan. As discussed, it also stands opposed to governmental or majoritarian efforts to compel orthodoxy with regard to the rights of homosexuals, the right to abortion, or any other matter supported by the political left.

The First Amendment counsels that society benefits when we engage with one another on matters of public concern and not seek to force one another to bend the knee. Compulsion and coercion are misguided means of "winning" arguments about patriotism or faith. In any event, by their nature, these arguments are not winnable. The fundamental lesson of the anti-orthodoxy principle is that within some narrowly prescribed limits, each of us gets to decide whether and how we honor the flag and how we will pray, dress, speak, and communicate our viewpoints.

4

The Public Forum

[I]n an open democratic society the streets, the parks, and other public places are an important facility for public discussion and political process. They are in brief a public forum that the citizen can commandeer; the generosity and empathy with which such facilities are made available is an index of freedom.[1]

The Supreme Court has observed that First Amendment rights require "breathing space" for their effective exercise.[2] That "breathing space" can take the form of doctrinal rules, such as those concerning defamation (see chapter 1), which expand opportunities for expression concerning matters of public concern. However, it also comes in the form of access to public places or properties, including properties that are used for engaging in First Amendment rights of speech and assembly.

This chapter focuses on place and its relationship to dissent and democracy.[3] One manner in which authorities can quiet or quell dissent is to restrict access to physical or now, in the digital era, cyber-places in which speech and assembly occur. Restricting access to these places limits the ability of individuals and groups to communicative grievances to public and official audiences. When access to government officials is restricted, this reduces opportunities for interactions between the governors and the governed.

Governments have historically exercised broad control over access to public places such as streets and parks. Indeed, initially that authority was unbridled—like private property owners, officials could deny access to public places for any reason or no reason at all. By the 1950s and 1960s, as the civil rights movement was demonstrating the importance of public places to communicating dissent, the Supreme Court's First Amendment doctrines were beginning to recognize rights of access to such places. The very concept of the "public forum"—a public property that is open and

The First Amendment in the Trump Era. Timothy Zick.
© Timothy Zick 2019. Published 2019 by Oxford University Press.

available for the purpose of exercising First Amendment rights—is rooted in conflicts over access to public places for the purpose of communicating about civil rights.

Recognition of access rights in at least some public places was a critically important development for First Amendment rights and American democracy. However, it did not guarantee adequate "breathing space" for public discourse and dissent. In fact, conflicts relating to access to public forums and rights of public expression have been a persistent theme of the First Amendment's history and tradition. As they have in the past, conflicts over access to public places have flared up during the Trump Era. Governmental attitudes toward, and responses to, public protests have once again raised concerns about the vitality of the public forum and the provision of "breathing space" for the public exercise of First Amendment rights.

An important new wrinkle has also appeared in the present era. The president's use of Twitter has raised novel questions concerning the extent to which the public has a right to communicate in the spaces of what the Supreme Court recently referred to as the "modern public square"—the internet and social media.[4] This is a Trump-specific concern, but it is also a critical issue of the Trump Era—whether speakers have access rights to social media sites used by government officials is an open issue that courts are only just beginning to decide. As governments and public officials make more frequent use of social media platforms to reach constituents and other audiences, important access questions will continue to arise. During the Trump Era and thereafter, access to digital public forums will become an increasingly important First Amendment concern.

Public Protest and Dissent in the Trump Era

Candidate Trump proclaimed that he was the "law and order" candidate and that he would be a "law and order" president.[5] Historically, that proclamation and label have not boded well for public protests, demonstrations, and similar public forms of dissent. Governments have historically viewed public protests and other forms of public contention as significant threats to "law and order." They have frequently adopted suppressive measures to contain public contention.

Many factors, among them laws regulating public protests and demonstrations, restrictions on access to public places, and aggressive public policing methods have limited the exercise of First Amendment rights in public places. These obstacles exist in the Trump Era. Moreover, President Trump and other officials have derided public protests as a form of "mob rule." Predictably, officials have taken or proposed measures that would rein in public contention. In addition, as noted, methods such as blocking Twitter critics have similarly posed questions about the extent to which the government is allowed to suppress dissent in digital places.

President Trump's attitude toward public dissent was on clear display during his 2016 campaign rallies. During some of those rallies, candidate Trump told crowds that he was nostalgic for past eras, when vocal dissenters were "roughed up." He encouraged his supporters to physically remove protesters from rallies. After being assaulted at a rally that took place in Louisville, Kentucky, a group of protesters sued candidate Trump for "inciting a riot." A federal appeals court ruled that Trump was exercising his free speech rights and hence could not be held liable, in large part because the candidate urged supporters not to hurt the protesters.[6] (The First Amendment imposes a high bar for liability for advocacy of unlawful action, requiring that there be express advocacy of unlawful action and that the action be both imminent and likely to occur.)[7]

That he escaped personal liability should not obscure the fact that part of the "show" at the Trump rallies was to place dissenters in danger of being harmed by the audience (something that did in fact occur on certain occasions).This attitude toward even peaceful protest did not change after Trump was elected president. Indeed, from its earliest days, the Trump administration cracked down on public protest and dissent. Setting an early tone, the Department of Justice prosecuted a woman who laughed (involuntarily, she claimed) at the confirmation hearing of Jefferson Sessions to be attorney general of the United States. The woman was tried and convicted of disorderly conduct and "demonstrating" on the U.S. Capitol grounds. For her audacious act of public dissent, she faced a hefty fine and up to a year in prison. Prosecutors finally dropped the case, but only after winning a jury verdict that was tossed out by the trial judge and initially announcing their intention to retry the case.[8] Like the campaign rallies, the case foreshadowed the administration's subsequent approach to public acts of dissent.[9]

A more troubling action was taken by the Department of Justice shortly after President Trump's inauguration. The Department prosecuted a group of more than 200 individuals who participated in inaugural day protests in January 2017. Using a form of "command and control" policing, law enforcement officials "kettled" hundreds of inaugural protesters by surrounding and physically restricting their movement. During its investigation of the case, the government sought unprecedented access to digital records relating to protest organizing and participation. It ultimately charged a large group of protesters with several felony counts of "conspiracy to engage in a riot."[10] After it failed at the first of several planned trials to demonstrate that the named defendants had actually engaged in any unlawful activity, the government was forced to drop the remaining charges.

As President Trump began to weigh in on public protests and the administration began to adopt policies that affected protest policing, some other implications of the "law and order" agenda began to emerge. As noted in chapter 3, the president proposed that flag-burning be criminalized and flag burners denaturalized. The president also refused to condemn the use of violence against public protesters at the Turkish Embassy in Washington, DC.[11] Further, in the wake of Black Lives Matter protests across the nation, the Federal Bureau of Investigation listed "black identity extremism" as a domestic terrorism threat.[12]

Later, President Trump labeled protests that erupted at Supreme Court nominee Bret Kavanaugh's confirmation hearing "embarrassing." In public comments, he asked why such protests were even allowed to occur. Like several Republican senators, President Trump adopted the view that the anti-Kavanaugh demonstrations, many of which occurred in the corridors of Congress, were staged by Democratic activists in an effort to impose "mob rule."

As one might expect of a "law and order" administration, the Trump administration has steadfastly supported law enforcement, including with regard to efforts to police public protests and demonstrations. Reversing an Obama Era policy, the Trump administration provided significant federal funds for equipment, including military vehicles, which could be used to quell public protests and demonstrations.[13] The prior policy had been adopted out of a concern that aggressive and militarized policing would exacerbate public safety concerns and suppress First Amendment rights at public protests and demonstrations.

In short order, the "law and order" agenda filtered down to state lawmakers. Subsequent to the Trump inaugural protests and some other high-profile protests, many state legislatures proposed laws to sharply curtail public protests. The measures included the following:

- Making it a felony to block a highway;
- Significantly increasing the amount of civil fines for obstructing traffic or trespassing;
- Authorizing police to shut down public protests, including by "any means necessary;"
- Making it a crime to leave an "unlawful assembly;"
- Allowing businesses to sue individuals who target them with protests;
- Increasing fines for "mass picketing" behavior;
- Prohibiting the wearing of masks, robes, or other disguises during public protests and demonstrations;
- Permitting localities to charge protesters for the costs of policing events;
- Exempting drivers from civil liability if they strike protesters under certain circumstances;
- Pursuing protesters under anti-racketeering laws, including asset forfeiture provisions;
- Making it a crime to threaten, intimidate, or retaliate against current or former state officials; and
- Requiring public community colleges and universities to expel any student convicted of participating in a violent riot.[14]

To be sure, these and similar proposals did not originate with the Trump administration. However, they directly followed high-profile public protests, including those that occurred at Trump's inaugural.[15] Whether or not they were a coordinated response, the measures are certainly consistent with the Trump administration's "law and order" agenda.

Civil libertarians cried foul, claiming that the proposals were efforts to stifle dissent. In one sign of the changing world order during the Trump Era, the United Nations published a report claiming that *U.S. lawmakers* were jeopardizing basic human rights relating to freedom of speech and assembly.[16] For a variety of reasons, likely including concerns that some of the proposals violated the First Amendment, most of these measures did not become law. However, they were a clear shot across the bow, particularly to Black Lives Matter, environmental, and other groups that rely on public protests to communicate their messages.

Consistent with this general attitude toward public protest and dissent, the National Park Service proposed new limits on public protests and demonstrations on the National Mall and near the White House. Among other things, these rules would prohibit protests and demonstrations on the sidewalk near the White House, impose new restrictions in other areas on the National Mall where protests typically occur, and require that demonstrators pay fees to cover the security and other costs associated with policing demonstrations and protests. Like the other measures discussed, these rules would limit protest by adding several new restrictions to an already complex maze of permit and other requirements applicable at or near the seat of the national government.

Opposition to public protest and dissent has also affected use of the president's Twitter account. As the Supreme Court recently observed, social media and the internet more broadly constitute a "modern public square."[17] Increasingly, these are among the places where individuals engage with one another and with their governments. Presidents have long sought to leverage new technologies—radio, television—for the purpose of bypassing the press and communicating directly with the public. President Trump has relied even more significantly than his predecessors have on communications technology, in particular social media. He has used his Twitter account to reach an audience of many millions, in many cases in order to communicate official policies and trumpet administration successes.

When he uses Twitter, the president has made it clear that he does not want to engage with some of his critics. He has blocked a number of individuals for criticizing him personally or taking issue with administration policies. The following replies to presidential tweets resulted in the commenter being blocked from the president's Twitter account, which meant they were no longer able to reply to his comments:

- "To be fair you didn't win the WH: Russia won [the election] for you."
- A photo of Trump with the words superimposed on it, reading, "Corrupt Incompetent Authoritarian. And then there are the policies. Resist."
- An image of Pope Francis looking incredulously at Trump, along with the statement, "This is pretty much how the whole world sees you."
- "The same guy who doesn't proofread his Twitter handles the nuclear button."
- A tweet by President Trump that read "Congratulations! First new Coal Mine of Trump Era Opens in Pennsylvania," followed by a comment stating "Congrats and now black lung won't be covered under #TrumpCare."

- After President Trump tweeted a video of his weekly presidential address with the hashtag "#Weekly Address," a commenter responded "Greetings from Pittsburgh, Sir. Why didn't you attend your #PittsburgNotParis Rally in DC, Sir?"
- After the president tweeted, "The Justice Dept. should ask for an expedited hearing of the watered down Travel Ban before the Supreme Court—& seek much tougher version!" a commenter responded: "Trump is right. The government should protect the people. That's why the courts are protecting us from him."

President Trump has not denied that he (and an official who assists him with the Twitter account) blocked these individuals based solely on the negative and critical content of their replies. Whether blocking critics from the comments section of the president's Twitter page violates the First Amendment is now up to the courts. However they answer that question, blocking critics from an important part of the "modern public square" undoubtedly diminishes the "breathing space" for public dissent.

The recognition that speakers and assemblies have a right to access public properties has been critically important to American public discourse and democracy. President Trump is certainly not the first public official to fail to appreciate the First Amendment significance of access to the public forum for the purpose of protesting, demonstrating, and dissenting. The Trump Era provides yet another important opportunity to revisit the reasons why preserving expressive access in public places, including government social media sites, is necessary to preserving a culture of dissent.

The Democratization of Dissent

The First Amendment's text mentions rights of speech, assembly, and petition. Effective exercise of each of these rights depends, in significant part, on access to public properties that facilitate communication, association, and presentation of grievances to government officials. However, for much of American history, speakers and assemblies did not have First Amendment rights to access public properties such as streets and parks. Like the other rights in the Bill of Rights, the First Amendment, which begins "Congress shall make no law . . . ," was not interpreted such that it applied to the states until the mid-1920s. As we will see, even after the First Amendment was enforced against the states and localities, they continued to exercise broad legal authority over access to public properties.

In colonial America, the lack of formal rights to access public properties for expressive purposes did not prevent the people from using these places to speak, assemble, and petition government. In the colonies, the people gathered in town squares and other public places. The colonists frequently engaged in public demonstrations, parades, marches, and boycotts.[18] They gathered in streets and town squares, often around "Liberty Trees" and "Liberty Poles," to protest taxation and other perceived abuses of British authority. These events typically involved chanting, marching, and hanging or burning political figures in effigy.[19]

These collective displays were among the earliest forms of American political discourse. They were the seeds of what would later become the robust freedoms of speech, assembly, and association. Public protests and demonstrations democratized dissent. They involved members of the public who could not afford to print or purchase pamphlets and broadsides, or perhaps had difficulty following the sometimes complex arguments presented in those forms.[20] Parades, pickets, boycotts, and demonstrations expanded and magnified the voice of the people. They created the first real "breathing space" for the exercise of expressive rights.

Public demonstrations and other events were efficacious means of political resistance and dissent. They were critical to the ultimate defeat of measures including the infamous Stamp Act, which required that colonists use only paper approved by Parliament to memorialize contracts and conduct commerce. Assemblies in the streets of New York City, Boston, and other population centers sent a strong message to local and British authorities that the colonies would not tolerate taxation without representation.[21]

Insofar as public officials were concerned, reports of mass demonstrations were often of greater concern than the explosion of broadsides and newspaper editorials. The latter forms communicated elite concerns to educated audiences. By contrast, demonstrations and parades communicated *mass* discontent. They did so in tangible, visible, and powerfully symbolic ways that newspaper columns and pamphlets could not replicate.

Demonstrations and other forms of public dissent facilitated and propelled the American Revolution. Early lessons in mass democracy were not lost on subsequent generations. Public demonstrations and parades were significant aspects of "out of door" politics for both supporters and opponents of the proposed Constitution, and later for proponents and opponents of the abolition of slavery.[22] Democratic modes of dissent were also a central aspect of post-Founding politics. In the nineteenth century, a variety of ethnic, religious, labor, and other groups used demonstrations, parades, and pickets to advance their causes.[23] Workers, the poor, racial minorities, and a variety of social movements relied on collective forms of expression to force policymakers and the public at large to give them a hearing.

Some evidence suggests that nineteenth century Americans were generally supportive of public dissent, thus lending it further democratic legitimacy.[24] Although, as noted, the First Amendment's protections for freedom of speech, assembly, and petition had not yet been applied against state and local governments, Americans asserted rights to assemble and speak in public places anyway. They participated in festivals, parades, and other collective activities. In general, during much of early American history, the people had relatively broad access to the streets and other public places for the purpose of demonstrating, marching, and engaging in other democratic forms of politics.

Notably, during the nineteenth century, permit requirements and other now-ubiquitous bureaucratic restrictions on parades and other assemblies had not yet materialized. Officials were empowered to suppress unlawful assemblies, and to prevent and punish non-peaceable assemblies, including violent riots. Local officials frequently took measures to quell labor unrest and limit boycotts and pickets. However, during most of the nineteenth century, the general threshold for official intervention at political protests and demonstrations was relatively high. This afforded marchers, demonstrators, and protesters considerable latitude in terms of both being present in public places and engaging in contentious but nonviolent activities there.[25]

Like their colonial forebears, antebellum Americans generally considered demonstrations and other collective displays to be an effective means of political expression. Only a generation removed from the American Revolution's experience with the democratization of dissent, the public appeared to view rights of public speech and assembly as fundamental— even though the courts had not yet formally reached that conclusion.

The "Public Forum"

By the early twentieth century, both public attitudes and official latitude respecting public speech, assembly, and petition activities had started to change. There were increasing concerns about violence, disorder, and disruption. These could be traced in part to the violence that sometimes erupted during Civil War Era and other nineteenth century public events. This violence led to heightened restrictions on access to public streets, parks, and other properties. At the beginning of the twentieth century, the battle over access to and First Amendment rights in these places reached a critical juncture.

During the early twentieth century, members of the International Workers of the World (IWW) provoked "free speech fights" by asserting rights to speak and assemble on street corners and in other public places.[26] They challenged the use of designated "free speech zones," which limited and confined speakers in order to control their movements, activities, and communications. The "Wobblies," as IWW members were called, were among the first to assert a First Amendment *right* to assemble and communicate in the public streets. They did not often prevail on their constitutional arguments. However, their efforts highlighted the importance of public places to collective expression and democratic dissent.

The "free speech fights" also exposed a central fault line with respect to early conceptions of civil liberties. Despite America's long history of public demonstrations, parades, and other forms of collective expression, during the twentieth century public officials and courts began to exert greater control over public access to streets and other places. Permit requirements, which required speakers and assemblies to obtain the permission of government officials prior to being granted access to public streets and parks, became much more common. Some local authorities asserted and exercised the power to deny access for any reason whatsoever, including based on the content of the assembly's message.

By the dawn of the twentieth century, the notion that governments owned public places, and thus had a right, like any private owner, to deny access to them, had begun to gain a measure of official acceptance. In 1897, the Supreme Court affirmed the conviction of a preacher who had made a public address on Boston Common without first obtaining the permission of the city's mayor.[27] The Court concluded that as a property owner, the city had the *absolute* power to deny access to Boston Common. The decision provided states, localities, and lower courts with grounds for adopting and upholding measures limiting, and in some cases denying, access by speakers and assemblies to streets, parks, and other public properties.

However, in the 1930s, the Supreme Court suggested that its initial judgment with regard to public properties—that public officials had the same right to exclude exercised by private property owners—was in error. In *Hague v. Committee for Industrial Organization*, the Court invalidated a city ordinance that prohibited labor meetings from taking place in public.[28] Justice Roberts famously observed, *"Wherever the title of streets and parks may rest, they have immemorially been held in trust for the use of the public and, time out of mind, have been used for purposes of assembly, communicating thoughts between citizens, and discussing public questions."*[29]

Roberts's important observation connected America's history of collective expression with what would eventually become a right of access to certain public properties for the purpose of exercising First Amendment speech, assembly, and petition rights. *Hague* suggested that by "immemorially" asserting and exercising expressive rights in public places, Americans had preserved a fundamental right of access to the public streets and parks. Although *Hague* did not resolve the nature or extent of this access right, it rejected the idea that government had absolute power to exclude. The government, then, was not just like a private property owner. It could not simply eject the public from the streets and parks for whatever reason it wished or because it wished to suppress the speakers' messages.

Over the course of the next several decades, the Supreme Court would build out the First Amendment's "expressive topography"—the places where speakers and assemblies had a right to speak, assemble, and petition government.[30] Like the Wobblies before them, Jehovah's Witnesses and other speakers challenged restrictions that limited their ability to reach public audiences.[31] As these and other dissenters pushed for access to a variety of public properties, the Supreme Court began to develop First Amendment doctrines that recognized speech, assembly, and petition rights in certain categories of public places.[32]

The concept of the "public forum" was a central aspect of this construction project.[33] Rooted in *Hague*'s recognition that certain properties were held "in trust" for the public for the exercise of expressive rights, the "public forum" principle limited governmental power to regulate and restrict public expression. The "trust" recognized in *Hague* developed into an enforceable First Amendment right to access and even "commandeer" the "public forum."[34] As the First Amendment scholar Harry Kalven Jr. wrote at the height of the civil rights movement:

> [I]n an open democratic society the streets, the parks, and other public places are an important facility for public discussion and political process. They are in brief a *public forum* that the citizen can commandeer; the generosity and empathy with which such facilities are made available is an index of freedom.[35]

Professor Kalven recognized the need for "some commitment to order and etiquette."[36] However, he advocated minimal governmental regulation in the public forum.[37] Recognition of a First Amendment "easement" with respect to certain public places, along with the right to "commandeer" those places for the purpose of parading, demonstrating, and marching with others, suggested a revival of the democratic tradition of public speech and assembly.[38]

As Professor Kalven observed, access to the "public forum" furthers important democratic functions. As colonial Americans first demonstrated, use of public properties for expressive purposes is critical to "public discussion and political process." The ability to access and even "commandeer" such properties facilitates self-government and effective public dissent. As Kalven suggested, the extent to which government allows access to such properties represents an "an index of freedom"—a measure of the government's willingness to tolerate and even facilitate public criticism and debate. In other words, official attitudes and policies concerning expression in the "public forum" can be useful in assessing the government's commitment to public discourse and democratic processes.

Like the policies of its predecessors, the Trump administration's "law and order" agenda should be interpreted through this lens. Further, the concept of the "public forum" continues to govern access to public properties— including, notably, official social media pages.

Managing the "Public Forum"

Although the "public forum" concept was a significant advancement for free speech, assembly, and petition rights, its significant promise has not always been realized. Doctrinal, social, and legal influences have exposed the realities and limitations of supposed rights to "commandeer" public properties and use them for public discussion and democratic processes.

The current "expressive topography" is the product of two doctrinal developments. The first is the rigid categorization of "public forums."[39] Under the Supreme Court's categorical approach, speakers have the greatest First Amendment rights in "traditional" public forums such as public streets, parks, and most sidewalks. If the government intentionally opens other properties to a diversity of speakers and expressive activities (a rare occurrence), it creates "designated" public forums in which speakers can also assert relatively broad First Amendment rights. Finally, governments can create "limited" public forums in which expressive activity can be limited to certain topics or speakers. Private properties, including shopping malls and social media websites, are simply off the grid—in general, they are not considered to be part of the "expressive topography," and speakers have no First Amendment access rights in such places.[40]

The second important First Amendment doctrine allows the government to regulate the "time, place, and manner" of speech in the public forum.[41] Thus, in both "traditional" and "designated" public forums, governments can restrict expression in furtherance of content-neutral public safety, order, tranquility, and even aesthetic interests. However, they cannot impose content-based regulations—restrictions that target particular messages or viewpoints for exclusion. In "limited" public forums, governments can impose any "reasonable" regulation on expression, and may limit discussion to certain topics or specific classes of speakers so long as they do not target particular viewpoints. Professor Kalven once referred to these standards as a kind of "Roberts Rules of Order" for expression in the public forum—although, as we will see, they do far more than impose basic order.[42]

Although the rejection of the private property metaphor has benefitted a diversity of public speakers, the public forum doctrine has been roundly criticized.[43] Its rigid and confusing categorization framework distracts courts from vital First Amendment concerns and encourages them instead to parse tracts of land. With respect to most public properties, forum categorization results in limited or no First Amendment access rights. Many public places where speakers seek out an increasingly mobile citizenry— municipal airports, shopping centers and mega-malls, state fairgrounds, and plazas abutting buildings constructed with public funds but without any expressive "tradition"—are not considered public forums. Thus, speakers wishing to engage public audiences in these places do not have any First Amendment right to do so.

In the remaining places, the power and deference granted to public officials, including the authority to value not just order and safety but commerce and even aesthetics over the exercise of First Amendment rights, restricts opportunities for public expression. There are public safety and order risks associated with collective expression, particularly in the case of large-scale protests and demonstrations. The Supreme Court has observed "such united and joint action involves even greater danger to the public peace and security than the isolated utterances and acts of individuals."[44] Officials are often faced with the challenge of maintaining the public peace while protecting the people's right to engage in public speech, assembly, and petition.

One of the lessons of history is that the balance between public order and First Amendment rights has often disfavored the latter. Thus, even in places that are amenable to expressive activity, First Amendment rights have been sharply circumscribed pursuant to concerns about public safety and order (not to mention aesthetics and personal repose). Time, place, and manner regulations allow officials to restrict, divert, and displace speakers and assemblies in ways that can significantly diminish the effectiveness of public expression.[45]

For example, detailed permit requirements, which include restrictions on various aspects of collective expression, are a common feature of modern public forum management. Even small groups seeking to stage a demonstration or protest must sometimes navigate a gauntlet of permit regulations, advance notice requirements, fees, route restrictions, time and size limits, and conduct proscriptions.

First Amendment doctrines also allow governments to control public expression and contention through a variety of spatial and other tactics.[46] For example, they frequently establish "free speech zones" (a tactic first encountered by the Wobblies)—specific public areas in which demonstrators and speakers are authorized to assemble and communicate. Expressive zoning has been used during critical public events, including major political party conventions, summits of world leaders, and antiwar demonstrations.

Free speech zoning significantly circumscribe movement, which is obviously a critical component of events such as demonstrations and protests. It displace speakers, sometimes moving them beyond sight and sound of intended audiences. Zoning also marginalizes dissent, by forcing those assembled to file into pens and other structures that have been pre-approved by government officials. Zoning communicates to public audiences that protest and dissent are a threat to public safety. Finally, zoning and other limits on where collective expression can occur diminish the *vocality* of place—as, for example, when speakers or assemblies are displaced from symbolically potent buildings and target audiences.[47]

Although permit requirements, zoning, and other restrictions do not explicitly target the content of speech, they impose restrictions on public expression that are at least as problematic as content-based measures.[48] Despite these concerns, courts have generally upheld the government's authority to regulate collective and other forms of public expression through zoning and other spatial regulations.

Public forum and other First Amendment doctrines apply in a world characterized by the gradual shrinkage of the public space available for collective forms of expression.[49] A range of social factors have further limited opportunities for effective public expression. These include the privatization of formerly public properties, the construction of "business enterprise zones" in city centers, the proliferation of gated communities, the erection of security barriers around public buildings, and the closing of public parks.[50]

Public policing methods also have a significant impact on the exercise of public speech, assembly, and petition rights.[51] During the twentieth century, what political sociologists have referred to as "escalated force" policing was commonly used to manage contention in the public forum.[52]

Escalated force policing was used against labor agitators, civil rights protesters, anti-Vietnam War activists, and political protesters at the 1968 Democratic National Convention in Chicago. Under the escalated force approach, law enforcement officers would typically order crowds to disperse from public forums. If they refused, officers would immediately resort to the use of physical force and violence to manage the situation. During the 1960s and 1970s, as conflict spilled into the streets and onto the nation's campuses, protesters sometimes resorted to violence. Law enforcement escalated its response to all forms of public dissent.

This approach made public protest a dangerous, at times even deadly, event. It resulted in mass arrests, police brutality, and the deaths of protesters on the campus of Kent State University. During the "Battle of Chicago" at the 1968 Democratic National Convention, more than 1,000 people, including peaceful demonstrators, police, reporters, and residents who had nothing to do with the convention were injured.[53] This was what protest policing entailed at the time President Richard M. Nixon announced his own "law and order" agenda to the nation.

By the 1970s, many police forces in the United States had adopted a "negotiated management" approach to public demonstrations and other events.[54] Under this approach, participants and police representatives discussed the details of public events in advance—including the location or route, the number of participants, the manner of visual displays, and even arrest logistics in case anyone violated the law.

From the perspective of police forces, negotiated management reduced the chances that public events would result in significant disruption or violence. It provided police with advance notice of the location and size of events, which facilitated planning and improved safety. Although it produced these benefits, negotiated management reduced mobility, eliminated spontaneity, and distorted messages intended to convey opposition to authority.[55]

Starting before, but in a pronounced way after the September 11, 2001, terrorist attacks, authorities turned to a "command and control" approach to public policing. This approach is far more aggressive and invasive than negotiated management. Command and control emphasizes "'the micro-management of all aspects of demonstrations,'" including the use of restrictive permitting processes; efforts to control public space through the use of barricades, police lines, and other mechanisms to surround, subdivide, and direct the flow of protesters; and "'a willingness to use force against even minor violations of the law.'"[56] Police dress in riot gear, use military vehicles and weapons, and engage in surveillance of organizations prior to planned demonstrations and other events.

President Trump's decision to assist local police forces in the purchase of military-style policing equipment facilitates "command-and-control" protest policing. The "kettling" of large groups of protesters at Trump's inaugural festivities, and their indictment under "public riot" charges, are likewise manifestations of this kind of protest policing.

Efforts to manage expression in the public forum have highlighted the continuing struggle to balance rights to engage in public contention and the government's interest in maintaining "law and order." The great promise of the public forum has not generally been realized. Professor Kalven's "index of freedom" has been diminished by a combination of First Amendment doctrines that have bureaucratized management of public properties, social and constitutional architectures that have contracted the expressive topography, and public policing methods that have imposed order at the cost of collective expression.

Preserving the Public Forum

During the Trump Era, we are once again witnessing conflict at the intersection between "law and order" policies and attitudes and First Amendment rights in the public forum. In order to preserve the public forum for expressive uses, we must again face and overcome the challenges these policies and related attitudes pose for public protest and dissent. Further, it will also be critically important to deal with the challenges relating to dissent and expression in digital spaces—including restrictions on the ability to communicate with public officials on social media and in other places in the "modern public square."

Protest and Dissent in the Public Forum

President Trump and some of his supporters have expressed an open hostility toward public protests and demonstrations. Some of that hostility may stem from the violent and destructive nature of certain protests. Some of it may also be related to the recent spate of incidents in which those opposed to the Trump administration or its policies have protested and heckled administration officials—including while they patronized restaurants or other public places not related to their official responsibilities. Some may view this protest tactic as a form of harassment.

We need to separate First Amendment rights to use the public forum for lawful protest and dissent from concerns about these kinds of protest methods. Protesters who engage in violence and damage property can and should be punished. There is no First Amendment right to harass another, or to insist on access to them outside of public forums. However, recently officials have reacted to protest events not by focusing on holding lawbreakers accountable, but instead by seeking new and more severe ways to punish even peaceful and nonviolent forms of dissent or civil disobedience. Lawmakers should not use incidents of unlawful behavior as a cover for cracking down on public protests more generally. Similarly, whatever one thinks of the social propriety of protesting diners while they eat out, this method of dissent should not color how we view the exercise of speech and other First Amendment rights in public forums.

In some respects, official attitudes toward public dissent during the Trump Era resemble those prevalent during certain prior eras. Chapters 2 and 3 discussed official efforts to stifle dissent and "sedition" during wartime. For example, President Nixon decried antiwar protests as evidence of the death of civilization.[57] Again, however, the nation is not currently engaged in a declared war or wide-scale international conflict. Indeed, as discussed in chapters 2 and 3, part of what makes the Trump Era distinct is the extent to which protest and dissent have been targeted even in a time of relative peace.

When it comes to protests and other forms of dissent that might disrupt the status quo, even a little bit, lawmakers, regulators, and law enforcement officers have too often treated these activities as a threat to society and evidence of a turn toward "mob rule." Dissenters have been characterized as paid mercenaries with no agenda other than to create chaos and disruption. During the Trump Era, this has become a prominent official characterization of protesters and demonstrators.

As discussed, so-called "law and order" policies that discourage or suppress the exercise of speech, assembly, and petition rights in public forums diminish the "breathing space" required for effective self-government. To be sure, of late we have seen nothing like the abusive policing practices that were used to stifle dissent during the 1960s and 1970s "escalated force" era discussed earlier. However, the president's proposal to jail individuals guilty of no offense other than engaging in lawful forms of political dissent, his characterization of public protests as "embarrassing," and his insistence on orthodox methods of protest all disrespect a long tradition of public contention dating back to the American Revolution.

Further, in terms of actual policies, we know that arming and militarizing law enforcement is physically and otherwise dangerous to dissent. It exacerbates the problems we have experienced with so-called "command and control" policing methods, which today remain a central part of the "law and order" agenda.

If, as Professor Kalven suggested, the degree of access afforded to public forum properties is an "index of freedom," we ought to judge our leaders and our democracy in part by how free the people are to speak, assemble, and petition in public places. Any public official who proclaims that public protests and public dissent are "embarrassing" cannot possibly be aware of the long historical struggle to gain access to public properties for precisely these purposes or the connection between public contention and democratic self-government. In order to preserve what remains of the expressive topography, lawmakers, political leaders, and law enforcement officials will all need to commit themselves to adopting policies that facilitate these goals and values and reject agendas intended to stifle even peaceful forms of protest and civil disobedience.

These changes cannot be effectively pursued absent changes to public attitudes regarding protest and dissent. If we are not prepared to tolerate the occasional disruption and disquiet that public dissent sometimes produces, we stand little chance of preserving what remains of a proud American tradition of public protest and demonstration.

Some might argue that this tradition is not worth preserving, particularly in an era when speakers and audiences have mostly migrated online. (More on that topic in just a moment.) However, recent public protest movements in the United States including Occupy Wall Street, Black Lives Matter, and the March For Our Lives belie the claim that access to tangible public forums no longer matters to American democracy.

It is true that our daily communications now most frequently occur in the "modern public square" of social media and the internet These spaces may be necessary to support the project of democracy going forward, but they are not sufficient to do so. For one thing, as privately owned media, Facebook and other social media are not bound by the limits the First Amendment imposes on officials when they seek to regulate speech or restrict speaker access to more traditional physical places. Rights in such spaces are contractual, not constitutional.

Moreover, as anyone who has done both can attest, mounting a public demonstration and participating in an "online protest" are markedly different modes of expression. They differ in terms of their capacity to facilitate solidarity, symbolic and other forms of contention, and associational mission. In short, preserving traditional forms of access to public places remains critically important to the modern-day communication of public dissent. Thus, we must work to preserve access rights in the tangible places where the First Amendment constrains official discretion.

The preservation work that must be done involves reversing or resisting the doctrines, trends, attitudes, and other influences discussed earlier.

Courts need to be far more sensitive to the suppressive nature of even "content-neutral" time, place, and manner restrictions. Instead of finding new ways to restrict access to public properties, officials and regulators ought to adopt policies that allow any expression that is compatible with the normal uses of the properties in question. Public attitudes also need to change, to exhibit a greater degree of tolerance and even respect for the right to dissent openly and in public places. Finally, police need to abandon the "command-and-control" and other repressive practices that make public protest not only unattractive but downright dangerous.

This is a heavy workload, and it requires changes across judicial, law-making, and law enforcement institutions. However, if nothing is done, a once-proud tradition of democratic dissent will continue to fall prey to draconian "law and order" policies that stifle dissent in public places.

Digital Dissent

Although digital spaces are not adequate replacements for more traditional public forums, they are undeniably important to modern speech, press, and associational activities. Digitization has been a tremendous boon for expression. However, it has also engendered some unique challenges.

We have more outlets and means of public communication than at any other time in history. However, as we are learning, these opportunities come with certain costs. Chapter 1 discussed the negative effects of digitization on the institutional press. As discussed further in chapter 5, hateful speech thrives in digital spaces. Further, in a digitized environment, personal reputations can be decimated in a matter of seconds. Finally, as the 2016 presidential election showed, "fake news"—events or statements that did not actually occur but are reported as fact—have now gained a disturbing foothold in digital media.

If digital platforms are going to serve the interests of democracy, we will need to address all of these challenges. The press has already had to revise business plans in response to digitization. Unfortunately, many outlets have also changed the substance and style of reporting to cater to the sensationalist tendencies of the modern public square.

Facebook and other social media have taken initial steps to remove some hateful speech and speakers from their platforms. While these steps may make the platform more welcoming to minorities and less harmful to participants, they raise delicate questions about the extent to which private intermediaries will be able to control and restrict public discourse. President Trump and his allies have also presented questions about digital forms of partisanship or bias when it comes to things such as search results and social media policies. Those questions will continue to arise as companies take steps to restrict the communication of speech based on its content.

Proposals to combat "fake news" through direct regulation, compelled disclosure of sponsors, or other means will all raise very tricky First Amendment questions. Government officials, who unlike social media are bound by the free speech and press provisions of the First Amendment, will have to tread carefully when addressing the "truth" or "falsity" of online speech. Readers and social media participants will have to become smarter and more vigilant consumers of online news, or seek their news in places other than Facebook feeds and Twitter timelines. If social media are to perform the democratic functions of "the modern public square," all of these and other pressing matters will have to be addressed—both during and well after the Trump Era has ended.

As discussed earlier, one related and currently pressing concern of the Trump Era involves the extent to which the people will be able to reach their governmental representatives in digital spaces. Assuming President Trump has provided something of a communications model for the modern-day politician, what if any rights will people have to engage with officials in new digital forums?

As discussed earlier, President Trump has teed up that issue by blocking some Twitter commenters based on their communication of unflattering opinions or arguments. Whether blocking users from replying to his tweets in this context violates the First Amendment involves some complicated distinctions between the power of government officials to regulate private speech and their right to engage in speech—and all of this in what are typically viewed as *private* properties or platforms.

To simplify the arguments in the pending case, the government contends that President Trump's Twitter account is a private space where the president can communicate with a public audience of his own choosing. By contrast, the users who were blocked argue that the Twitter account, or at least that part of it that allows replies to the president's tweets, is the equivalent of a "digital town hall" where the president has thrown some attendees out owing solely to their political viewpoints.

A federal trial court has ruled that the "interactive space" of the president's Twitter account is a "designated public forum" as to which the First Amendment applies. The court relied on the fact that President Trump has used his Twitter account to announce foreign affairs policies and cabinet-level personnel decisions and that he has exercised official control over the account, rendering his blocking activity an official regulatory action subject to the First Amendment. Because he blocked users based on the negative viewpoints they had expressed in their replies, the court concluded that President Trump violated the First Amendment.

Among other things, the decision demonstrates the importance of the public forum concept even in a digital era. Commenters cannot insist that the president read their responses. However, in a public forum, they can insist that he not block their ability to engage with others who comment, respond, and retweet the president's communications. This is how discourse occurs in the "modern public square," and it is important that speech rights be preserved in such places. If it stands, the precedent will provide speakers with a basis for enforcing access rights to similar "official" social media accounts. It will also highlight the need to ensure that the channels of communication remain open and that dissent not be silenced—particularly when it is directed to government officials.

As this book goes to press, the Trump Twitter case is on appeal and it is possible that the trial court's decision will be reversed. That would be an unfortunate result insofar as digital dissent rights are concerned. As the Supreme Court recently emphasized, social media platforms such as Twitter offer "perhaps the most powerful mechanisms available to a private citizen to make his or her voice heard."[58] These platforms, the Court emphasized, permit citizens to "petition their elected representatives and otherwise engage with them in a direct manner."[59] As public officials increasingly use social media as a means of speaking to and hearing from their constituents, the First Amendment ought to safeguard the rights of citizens to participate freely in these virtual forums, including by expressing criticism and dissent.

If the district court's decision is reversed and the president's blocking stands, we will have further evidence that the "expressive topography" is shrinking in ways that undermine and indeed censor dissent. If the First Amendment does not apply in places where governments increasingly communicate and public discourse and dissent increasingly occur, the people will lose precisely the kind of "breathing space" that is required for effective digital dissent.

5

Dealing with "Hate Speech"

Speech that demeans on the basis of race, ethnicity, gender, religion, age, disability, or any other similar ground is hateful; but the proudest boast of our free speech jurisprudence is that we protect the freedom to express "the thought that we hate."[1]

Donald Trump has again thrust issues relating to "hate speech" into national public discourse. Indeed, one of the singular things about his candidacy and presidency is the extent to which Trump has himself participated in communicating derogatory views. Of course, long before there was a candidate or President Trump, America faced questions concerning how to deal with expression that denigrates or offends individuals based on race, gender, ethnicity, sexual orientation, and religion. Today we are facing this issue again on college campuses, in social media, and in public discourse more generally. Data indicate that hateful expression is on the rise. The president's own derogatory rhetoric may be connected to this phenomenon.

From the perspective of its targets, hateful and derogatory expression is associated with psychological, emotional, and physical harms. "Hate speech," as such expression is generally called, may also harm the body politic. Hateful statements that emanate from the president himself or his administration raise the stakes. Since they emanate from officialdom, they may implicate the equality, religious, and free speech rights of their targets. Further, some recent research has found a strong correlation between anti-Muslim hate crimes and President Trump's derogatory tweets about Muslims.[2] All of these concerns are amplified by social media, which assures that derogatory statements, in particular those emanating from a president with a global social media following, are echoed and broadcast widely.

For many Americans, given the harms associated with it and its seemingly low value, it is puzzling why the First Amendment protects "hate

The First Amendment in the Trump Era. Timothy Zick.
© Timothy Zick 2019. Published 2019 by Oxford University Press.

speech" at all. In many nations, including many industrialized democracies, "hate speech" is regulated or criminalized. However, under the First Amendment, "hate speech" is mostly protected speech—which is to say it cannot be targeted for suppression based on its derogatory content but can in narrow circumstances be restricted owing to its effects on physical safety and public order. Given the incidence and effects of hateful expression, we ought to be clear about the extent to which it is generally protected by the First Amendment and, more importantly, *why* it remains so. The Trump Era provides another opportunity to revisit this issue. It also provides another opportunity to consider the government's own role in communicating and combatting hate. We must consider not only the impact of private speech that denigrates, but also the effects of derogatory speech emanating from public officials.

Hate Speech in the Trump Era

Hateful and derogatory expression has long been an issue in American political and cultural discourse. Although Donald Trump certainly did not originate this concern, in a number of ways he has contributed to and exacerbated it.

From the beginning of his candidacy, Trump stoked racial, ethnic, religious, and other divisions in an effort to appeal to his political base. In public statements and frequent social media posts, he denigrated a wide variety of individuals and groups. Candidate Trump infamously denounced Mexican immigrants as "rapists" and "drug dealers." (He later accused a Mexican American judge of being biased, solely on the basis of his ancestry.) Candidate Trump openly mocked a disabled reporter. He made derogatory remarks about Muslims.

There is some evidence that during the 2016 presidential election, Russian operatives engaged in an orchestrated manipulation of social media in an effort to assist Trump's campaign. As part of that effort, operatives sought to sow or deepen racial divisions in the American electorate through the communication of derogatory ads. They posted and distributed ads denigrating Muslims, undocumented immigrants, and African Americans.

As president, Trump has continued to communicate in ways that derogate or insult based upon race, gender, and other characteristics. Most notably, he refused to denounce white supremacists who marched in Charlottesville,

Virginia, during the summer of 2017. Instead the president referred to some of those white supremacists as "very fine people" and denounced "both sides" for the violence that occurred on Charlottesville's streets. Thereafter, as the nation debated the moral and constitutional merits of openly displaying Confederate monuments, many of which were products of the racist Jim Crow era, President Trump expressed a strong desire to retain these monuments. While it may be hurtful and disappointing to many, his communication of support for Robert E. Lee and other Confederate icons is not itself a form of hateful expression. On the other hand, when the president has weighed in on the debate, he has not been clear about precisely *why* he holds his views.

The president has spoken more directly about race. On several occasions, he has publicly insulted the intelligence of African American lawmakers and professional athletes. President Trump has referred to certain African nations as "shitholes." On some occasions, he has described undocumented aliens as "animals."

Trump has cast a wide derogatory net. As a candidate and as president, Trump has made several derogatory remarks about both the appearance and intelligence of women. He and certain members of his administration have denigrated Muslims by suggesting that "Islam hates us" and is a "cancer." As a candidate, Trump called for a "total and complete shutdown of Muslims entering the United States"—a "Muslim ban," as he once proudly referred to it. As president, Trump has retweeted anti-Muslim propaganda videos.

The statements are troubling, coming as they do from the lips and social media account of the president. However, in part owing to their prominent source, these derogatory communications have caused significant harms to the body politic. Some view them as a license to openly use derogatory terms and communicate their own discriminatory beliefs—without regard to the serious consequences of this exercise of First Amendment rights. Since Trump's election, researchers have reported an increase in the number of incidents of xenophobic, racist, and homophobic speech directed to members of minority groups.

The Anti-Defamation League reported a 60 percent increase in anti-Semitic incidents in 2017.[3] Just days after the presidential election, a gay man in Michigan heard a taunt from a group of men: "Trump is going to get rid of people like you." A Jewish woman in Austin, Texas, said she heard the same threat from a middle-aged white man as she lined up to buy groceries. A black woman in Houston reported that she was told by a white man that

Trump was going to "get rid of all you n------." An Asian American woman in Hollywood, California, had her hair pulled by an older white woman and was told that she had to "go back to China" now that Trump is president.[4] In our social media era, many videos of whites harassing African Americans, Mexican Americans, and other racial and ethnic minorities have gone viral on social media.

Thus, it is not just the president's own speech that has raised concerns. Some supporters apparently view his election as a signal that "political correctness" no longer demands that they keep xenophobic and other derogatory remarks to themselves. A candidate who won with the overwhelming support of white voters and very little support from the groups being denigrated is looked upon by some as a standard-bearer who is fighting for those who feel their speech about race and religion has long been unduly chilled. There is also evidence that hate groups view the president's statements as supportive of their agendas. David Duke, a former Grand Wizard of the Ku Klux Klan, commented "[w]e are determined to take our country back. We are going to fulfill the promises of Donald Trump."

Since the election, the Trump administration has engaged with the issue of "hate speech" on the nation's campuses. During the past few years, invitations extended to white supremacists and other controversial speakers, as well as incidents of hateful expression by students and faculty, have roiled a number of American college and university campuses. This has stirred campus officials to comment publicly about the communication of hateful and derogatory ideas on campus and, in some instances, to consider imposing limits on such expression.

The Trump administration has strongly and publicly opposed such regulations. In public remarks, Attorney General Jefferson Sessions denounced them as a form of "political correctness" and criticized students who supported them as seeking shelter from ideas they did not like. During the Trump presidency, the Department of Justice has filed a number of "official statements" in federal lawsuits opposing campus harassment, bullying, and "hate speech" regulations.

Reacting in part to the debate about "hate speech" on campus, which includes alleged suppression of conservative viewpoints, in March 2019 the president issued an executive order that conditions the receipt of federal research funds at private and public universities on the protection of free speech on campus.[5] Tellingly, the president announced the order at a gathering of conservative activists, at which he linked the issue of free speech on campus to highly publicized incidents in which right-wing speakers had been excluded or attacked. At the signing ceremony, President Trump said, "Under the guise of speech codes, and safe spaces, and trigger warnings, these universities have tried to restrict free thought, impose total conformity and shut down the voices of great young Americans." He did not clarify whether the "great young Americans" referred to included figures such as Richard Spencer, a white supremacist who has been at the center of several controversies surrounding visits to college campuses.

"Hate Speech"—A Primer

Before analyzing the incidence of and response to "hate speech" during the Trump Era, it is helpful first to understand the current approach to this kind of expression under the First Amendment. Some commentators have asserted that "hate speech" is not protected speech. Others have insisted that any and all forms of hateful expression are fully protected under the First Amendment. Both of these perspectives are actually incorrect. In fact, *most but not all* hateful and derogatory speech is entitled to protection under the First Amendment. In other words, under current First Amendment doctrines and precedents, "hate speech" is (mostly) protected speech.

One of the first things to understand about "hate speech" is that the label lacks any independent First Amendment significance. Although First Amendment doctrines deal with certain defined categories of utterances, such as obscenity, incitement, and threats, "hate speech" is not among them.

There is no agreed-upon legal or constitutional definition of "hate speech." For purposes of this brief primer, we can adopt the legal philosopher Jeremy Waldron's definition: "[W]ords which are deliberately abusive and/or insulting and/or threatening and/or demeaning directed at members of vulnerable minorities, calculated to stir up hatred against them."[6] This definition describes the general class or category of speech we are considering.

Most of the speech in Professor Waldron's definition is protected by the First Amendment. Under long-standing First Amendment doctrines, government is generally not allowed to regulate speech based on the particular message or idea being communicated. The communication of hateful ideas falls within this general rule. The recognized exceptions to this content-neutrality principle are few and they are narrowly defined.

As mentioned, the Supreme Court has identified certain categories of speech that are not covered by the First Amendment at all. Insofar as the consideration of "hate speech" is concerned, the most relevant of these categorical exceptions are incitement to unlawful activity, "fighting words," and "true threats." Persistent forms of harassment are also not covered by the First Amendment.

Thus, speech that incites others to engage in unlawful activity is uncovered, but only if the speaker expressly advocates unlawful action and that action is both imminent and likely to occur.[7] Racial epithets and other abusive words can be punished as uncovered "fighting words," but only when they are directed to a specific person and are likely to result in an imminent breach of the peace (i.e., a brawl).[8] A "true threat" is a serious expression directed to a person or group of an intent to inflict bodily harm or death.[9] Finally, in order to fall outside the First Amendment, verbal and other forms of harassment must be persistent and produce serious interference with work, study, or other interests.

Note that under these exceptions, not every use of a racial, ethnic, or other slur is protected under the First Amendment. Hateful speech that meets any of these narrow definitions would not be covered by the First Amendment, and governments—including campus administrations—are allowed to regulate it. For example, inciting violence against particular Muslims would not be covered speech. Similarly, burning a cross with the intent to intimate or threaten an African American family is not protected speech under the First Amendment.[10] Pervasive harassment in the form of racially derogatory remarks is not protected speech.

However, it is important to understand that in each of these instances, the speech is considered beyond First Amendment bounds not because it contains a racial slur or other form of "hate speech," but rather because it is included within a categorical exclusion that is defined *without reference to* racist or other forms of hateful expression. Thus, the Supreme Court has emphasized that government generally cannot single out only certain fighting words, incitement, threats, etc. based upon their racist or other derogatory content.[11] In sum, the speech in these examples is categorically excluded from coverage not because it expresses hate but rather owing to the likelihood it will incite violence, or threaten physical injury, or negatively affect workplace or school-related functions.

Under these First Amendment standards, the various statements of candidate and now-president Trump concerning ethnic, racial, and religious minorities are all protected by the First Amendment. Even if it is intended to stir up hatred for targeted individuals and groups, speech that denigrates or insults Mexicans, African Americans, LGBT persons, women, or Muslims is not considered to be outside the domain of the First Amendment. Whether communicated by a government official or a private citizen, the idea that Mexicans are rapists or that Muslims are terrorists is entitled to First Amendment protection—even though the statements are offensive and hurtful overgeneralizations. Under this approach, hateful ideas and opinions communicated by white supremacists and other campus speakers are also protected under the First Amendment. Of course, that does not mean the ideas communicated by the president or the white supremacist cause no harm or pose no danger to individuals or society. It means that as currently interpreted, the First Amendment protects the remarks *despite* these harms.

Some of my examples of private speech, in particular those involving face-to-face communication of racial epithets, might be considered "fighting words." An individual who uses the N-word in a face-to-face altercation may not be allowed to fall back on the First Amendment when arrested for breach of peace or disorderly conduct. A student who persists in dogging a classmate and spewing racial or ethnic epithets can be punished under a student code of conduct for such actions. And a person who threatens another with physical injury can be held liable for the threat. But again, the reason for these carve outs has nothing to do with the racial or other derogatory content and everything to do with the danger to individual or communal safety.

So the First Amendment generally protects a speaker's right to communicate abusive, insulting, demeaning, and derogatory remarks. Fraternity members who sing racially offensive songs on campus cannot be expelled solely for their choice of language. A speaker who expresses the view that Mexican Americans or Asian Americans should "go back where they came from" is shielded by the First Amendment from official sanction. Anti-Semitic, racist, xenophobic, misogynistic, and other hateful speech is mostly protected by the First Amendment.

The First Amendment's protection for hateful and derogatory speech of this nature is truly exceptional. In Western democracies, hateful and derogatory speech is generally banned or regulated. Denmark bans statements "by which a group of people are threatened, derided or degraded because of their race, colour of skin, national or ethnic background." Germany prohibits attacks on the "human dignity of others by insulting, maliciously maligning or defaming segments of the population." In the United Kingdom, laws ban the use of "threatening, abusive or insulting words or behavior" when these are intended "to stir up racial hatred" or when "having regard to all the circumstances racial hatred is likely to be stirred up thereby." Canada prohibits any public statements that "incite hatred against any identifiable group where such incitement is likely to lead to a breach of the peace."[12]

These approaches to "hate speech" give primacy to interests such as individual equality and dignity. Laws in the nations mentioned, and others, permit government to pursue those interests by targeting and restricting hateful speech based on its content. By contrast, the First Amendment's protection for even derogatory speech calculated to stir up racial and other forms of hatred is predicated on the primacy of freedom of speech. As Justice Oliver Wendell Holmes Jr. observed, the First Amendment protects even "the thought that we hate."

"Hate Speech" and Harm

Having won the First Amendment battle and the right to communicate hateful ideas, purveyors of "hate speech" are too often prone to dismiss objections to its communication as mere "political correctness." Owing to the outsized influence freedom of speech has in our culture, too little time is spent considering the significant harms associated with hateful and derogatory speech. To better understand the implications of the First Amendment's current protection for hateful and derogatory speech, we ought to be familiar with the psychological, physical, political, and constitutional harms that such speech can cause.[13]

To understand the variety of harms that can be associated with hateful expression, consider the infamous request by a Nazi group to march in Skokie, Illinois. In the 1970s, a group of American Nazis applied for a permit to march in the town of Skokie, Illinois, in full Nazi regalia. At the time, Skokie was home to hundreds of Jews who had survived the Holocaust.

Town officials adopted several regulations designed to prevent the march from occurring. They argued, in part, that the Nazi march would cause severe psychological distress for some of the town's residents.[14] Ultimately, state and federal courts did not find the town's concerns about psychological harms sufficient to support suppressing the march and invalidated its regulations on First Amendment grounds.[15]

Skokie officials did not rely on the possibility of physical violence as a basis for suppressing the Nazi march. However, as the nation has recently witnessed, derogatory speech can indeed lead to actual physical violence. Three individuals lost their lives in Charlottesville. Hateful expression communicated via social media can also lead to acts of physical violence. As mentioned earlier, one study has discovered a strong correlation between President Trump's anti-Muslim tweets and incidences of violent hate crimes against Muslims in certain areas of the nation—in particular, those with high Twitter usage.[16]

Social media use may increase political and other forms of polarization, which thrive in online "echo chambers."[17] The study's authors concluded that the president's tweets, which were broadcast on social media to millions, led to an unprecedented increase in violent attacks on Muslims. Although polarization and anti-Muslim sentiment both preceded Trump's presidency, the study concluded that there was a discernible "Trump effect" in terms of online "hate speech" and hate crimes. They described these findings as "consistent with the interpretation that Trump's presidential campaign aided an unraveling of social norms that made people more willing to express views that were previously deemed socially unacceptable" and the conclusion that social media may have had a "non-negligible" effect on the translation of "hate speech" into hate crimes.[18]

Other types of physical harms can occur, for instance if the target of hateful speech lashes out at the speaker. Although the town did not rely on the danger of violent audience reactions against Nazi marchers, Skokie's lawyers argued that the display of the swastika was the equivalent of a physical attack on Holocaust survivors. If the speaker's words or expressive acts meet the definition of "fighting words," they are not covered by the First Amendment. As noted, the "fighting words" category protects the speaker and society from imminent brawls. However, in the Skokie case, the marchers' words and symbols would not have met the definition of "fighting words" because they would not have been directed to an individual with the intent of inciting an imminent brawl. Nor would they have constituted "true threats"—serious expressions of an intent to harm the town's residents. This demonstrates both the narrowness of the categorical exclusions and the scope of protection afforded to "hate speech."

Whether or not hateful and derogatory speech leads to individual hate crimes or acts of physical violence, as it permeates society this kind of expression can have deleterious effects on political communities. As Professor Waldron has argued, hateful and derogatory speech imposes significant political harms. Waldron starts from the premise that in a "well-ordered society" not only must all people be protected by the law, but they are entitled to live in confidence of this protection.[19] He argues, "Each person . . . should be able to go about his or her business, with the assurance that there will be no need to face hostility, violence, discrimination or exclusion by others."

Hateful expression undermines this public good. As Waldron explains: "When a society is defaced with anti-Semitic signage, burning crosses and defamatory racial leaflets," any expectation of security "evaporates." The objects of hateful and derogatory speech are deprived of the assurance that the society regards them as people of equal dignity.

Waldron continues: "In its published, posted or pasted-up form, hate speech can become a world-defining activity, and those who promulgate it know very well—this is part of their intention—that the visible world they create is a much harder world for the targets of their hatred to live in." He describes the implicit message of some of the "hate speech" incidents described earlier as follows:

I know you think you are our equals. But don't be so sure. The very society you are relying on for your opportunities and your equal dignity is less than whole-hearted in its support for these things, and we are going to expose that half-heartedness and build on that ambivalence every chance we get. So: think about it and be afraid. The time for your degradation and your exclusion by the society that presently shelters you is fast approaching.[20]

In sum, Professor Waldron argues that the basis for restricting hateful and derogatory speech is not that it leads to psychological or physical harms—although it may. Rather, in his view, the principal reason such expression ought to be restricted is that it produces an environment in which certain individuals in society must live in constant fear of being excluded or marginalized within that society. This harm cuts much deeper and is far more fundamental than merely being "offended" by racially derogatory words. In other words, political derogation or exclusion is a far cry from "political correctness."

Finally, hateful expression may produce constitutional harms. In particular, some have argued that the equal protection rights of persons in historically disadvantaged groups are put at risk by "hate speech."[21] This can be true whether it is the government itself communicating hateful messages, or private individuals creating an environment in which equal protection under law is only possible for some members of society. Thus, some proponents of "hate speech" regulation argue that since equality is a precondition of other rights, including the freedom of speech, it follows that racial and other stigmatizing speech ought not to receive First Amendment protection.[22]

In an era in which many believe that the president holds and espouses racist views, and some of his supporters interpret his words as licensing the communication of hateful messages, these psychological, physical, political, and constitutional concerns have become more acute. If the war on "political correctness" means that our society will become more outwardly racist, xenophobic, and otherwise dignity-disregarding, then we must again consider whether and how the First Amendment's protection of "hate speech" can be reconciled with the considerable harms it causes.

Why Protect "Hate Speech"?

Given these significant harms, why does the First Amendment generally protect hateful and demeaning expression? In an era in which "hate speech" appears to be proliferating in public spaces and on social media what explanation can one give, in particular to those who are targets of this kind of expression?

One approach we ought not to take is to minimize, mock, or politicize their concerns. Unfortunately, that has been the primary tactic of the Trump administration. The president's own statements are defended by the White House and its supporters as either benign or attacks on "political correctness." The administration and its allies have attacked campus "radicals" and "bureaucrats" who, they say, are engaged in a conspiracy to suppress *all* conservative opinions and viewpoints. This, incidentally, sounds a lot like the conspiracy theory that has led the president to suggest that Google's search algorithms ought to be "looked into" based on their supposed political bias.

It is an unfortunate reality that *both* right-wing and left-wing speakers have been singled out and effectively silenced—including on college campuses. Many recent conflicts involving campus speech have centered on the communication of "hate speech" by so-called "conservative" speakers. However, to assert that "radicals" and "bureaucrats" are engaged in some program of partisan oppression downplays the nature and scope of concerns raised when, for example, an avowed white supremacist is invited to a university campus. Even putting aside security and cost concerns that may arise in such instances, whether "white supremacy" is a viewpoint that students or faculty ought to invite into their campus communities and devote significant resources toward presenting is a complex question that involves considerations of both freedom of speech and academic freedom.[23]

To be sure, there have been some instances of wrong-headed suppression of even non-hateful expression by conservative groups and speakers. Those instances should be condemned. However, they should not obscure the concerns relating to the presence of white supremacist and other right-wing provocateurs on campus.

The Trump administration has sometimes downplayed the harms that this sort of "hate speech" can cause. For example, when he was attorney general, Jefferson Sessions described college students who raised concerns about "hate speech" on campus as "a generation of sanctimonious, sensitive, supercilious snowflakes." That sort of stereotyping and partisan rhetoric ignores the real and tangible effects of hateful and derogatory speech on college campuses and in other contexts. Indeed, it essentially denies that such harms exist, or that there is anything to debate. More importantly, statements such as this do nothing to explain why the First Amendment has been, and should continue to be, interpreted in a manner that protects the communication of derogatory and demeaning ideas and viewpoints. The attorney general's rhetoric is not a defense of the First Amendment. It is, rather, an attack on those who dare to question its scope.

To be sure, in some other contexts, the administration has done a better job of reminding the public of the First Amendment justifications for generally protecting "hate speech" despite the harms it inflicts. For example, in "statements of interest" filed in federal court cases challenging restrictions on the free speech rights of university students, faculty, and staff, the government has relied on traditional rules of content-neutrality and concerns about governmental suppression of viewpoints. It has opposed disciplinary provisions that target speech based on its content and other measures that restrict opportunities to engage in robust debate on campus. As Attorney General Sessions also observed at a forum on free speech in the context of higher education, "This country protects noisome assembly, immoderate speech and provocative speech. Whether left or right. Suppression of competing voices is not the American way." Sessions continued: "As Americans, we know it's far better to have a messy and contentious debate than to suppress the voices of dissenters."

These kinds of statements may not convince the targets of "hate speech" that the First Amendment ought to allow racist or other forms of bigoted expression. However, they at least hint at substantive explanations based on fundamental First Amendment doctrines and principles.[24]

As Nadine Strossen recently explained in her book defending the current First Amendment approach to "hate speech," allowing the government to decide which viewpoints are fit for consumption "would be a license for witch hunts" and install "a legal regime that enables officials to silence their critics."[25] Such an approach would allow government officials to determine the type of dissent and political expression deemed acceptable. That sort of power would be fundamentally incompatible with the values of self-governance, truth-seeking, and autonomy that undergird the First Amendment.

As discussed in chapter 3, the notion that government cannot target certain ideas, opinions, or viewpoints is a core premise of the First Amendment. As noted, this content-neutrality principle prohibits the imposition of official orthodoxy with respect to matters of public concern—including those relating to race, gender, religion, and undocumented status. Allowing government to single out certain statements or communications—outside the narrow categories of uncovered speech discussed earlier, which raise special concerns about imminent disorder or violence—would create the possibility of a mandated official orthodoxy concerning these matters.

During the 1980s and 1990s, concerns about the individual and communal harms associated with "hate speech" led municipalities and universities to adopt anti-bias "hate speech" provisions. The City of St. Paul, Minnesota, adopted an anti-bias ordinance that prohibited cross burnings and other expressive activities that would "arouse anger, alarm, or resentment in others *on the basis of race, color, creed, religion, or gender*."[26] The City of Indianapolis adopted an ordinance that provided a procedure for challenging and suppressing certain depictions of women that were considered misogynistic.[27] Many university campuses adopted "speech codes" that purported to ban hateful and derogatory communications by students, faculty, and staff.[28]

These measures were all responses to the psychological, physical, political, and constitutional harms described earlier. Governments sought to protect racial and ethnic minorities who were being threatened by cross burnings and other hateful public expression, women subjected to diminished status and societal harms from derogatory depictions of the female body, and students of color who were confronted with expression that interfered with their ability to pursue an education on equal terms and in an inclusive environment. However, all of these provisions were invalidated on First Amendment grounds—many because they singled out certain symbolic acts, communications, and depictions based on the subject matter or viewpoint conveyed.

The First Amendment does not permit government to select the sentiments or ideas speakers can convey—even with respect to matters of race, ethnicity, and gender. Some might object that there are no real ideas or opinions in "hate speech," and that the only content at issue is a derogatory insult that is not worthy of any First Amendment concern. Putting aside the question of how to narrow the definition of "hate speech" such that it *only* captures derogatory insults (which may already be unprotected "fighting words"), even hateful speech can be connected to commentary on matters of public concern.

For instance, in *Snyder v. Phelps*,[29] the Supreme Court overturned a civil verdict against the Westboro Baptist Church, whose members picket and protest near the funerals of military personnel killed in action. Church members carry signs communicating hateful views concerning gay men and lesbians, Catholics, the military, and the United States. The Court overturned a jury's verdict, which was based on the severe emotional distress inflicted on Matthew Snyder's father. It concluded that the signs conveyed opinions on "matters of public concern," including the military's then-enforced "Don't Ask, Don't Tell" regulations regarding the service of gays and lesbians in the armed forces and the Catholic Church's pedophilia scandal. As the Court explained:

Speech is powerful. It can stir people to action, move them to tears of both joy and sorrow and—as it did here—inflict great pain. [W]e cannot react to that pain by punishing the speaker. As a Nation we have chosen a different course—to protect even hurtful speech on public issues to ensure that we do not stifle public debate.[30]

The result in *Snyder* is admittedly a hard pill for some to swallow. Why bother protecting such deeply offensive and derogatory expression? The Court concluded that even "hate speech" can touch on ideas or opinions the public needs to hear about in order to make informed decisions about important matters. Where speech about race, religion, or sexual orientation relates to matters of public concern—that is, affirmative action, moral issues, or government policies—it is protected so that speakers and audiences can freely communicate about those things.

That does not give speakers a license to insult or harass. Less noticed, but also significant, were the limits the *Snyder* Court suggested for the communication of the Church's derogatory speech. The Court interpreted the speech as concerning several matters of public import. Thus, it did not consist merely of slurs or insults, some of which may be actionable under personal injury or other laws. Moreover, the Court made clear that government officials could regulate the time, place, and manner of funeral protests to ensure that they did not interfere with the funeral itself.

In general, though, enforcement of "hate speech" laws or codes interferes with the search for truth and citizens' own self-government—two of the primary justifications for protecting freedom of speech. The basic premise of the "marketplace in ideas" is that ideas and viewpoints ought to compete for societal acceptance. In the words of Justice Oliver Wendell Holmes Jr., "the best test of truth is the power of the thought to get itself accepted in the competition of the market."[31] As the Supreme Court has observed, "there is no such thing as a false idea."[32] Thus, "[h]owever pernicious an opinion may seem, we depend for its correction not on the conscience of judges and juries but on the competition of other ideas."[33] As Justice Brandeis put it, "the fitting remedy for evil counsels is good ones."[34] Thus, insofar as they express ideas or opinions rather than invite brawls or threaten the physical safety of others, even derogatory or offensive communications are part of the marketplace of ideas.

Further, insofar as governments are authorized to dictate acceptable viewpoints with regard to race, gender, religion, or other matters of public concern, this prevents democratic self-government. When the government bans or restricts certain speech owing to its perceived societal or political harms, it interferes with the robust public discourse and debate that voters and citizens rely on in a democratic system to address these effects. By censoring certain words, messages, and ideas, "hate speech" laws and speech codes can distort public discourses and debates relating to a host of issues: immigration, social justice, gender equality, and a variety of other matters of public concern

A long history of official suppression of dissent demonstrates that government enforcement of "hate speech" laws can also have a powerful chilling effect. It may be somewhat difficult at first to see hateful and derogatory communications as a form of "dissent." After all, dissent is typically associated with *minority* speakers or ideologies, and the purveyors of "hate speech" seem intent on entrenching majority power by denigrating and excluding racial, ethnic, and other minorities.

However, restricting "hate speech" affects dissenters' rights in several respects. While it is true that hateful speakers may wish to suppress the rights of minorities, not all "hate speech" is intended to have this effect. For example, a broad definition of "hate speech" would capture within its terms minority opinions about same-sex marriage, the relationship between Islam and terrorism, and the status or rights of undocumented immigrants. In those instances, governmental censorship may be used to suppress fringe, minority, or unpopular opinions.

Indeed, this is precisely what has occurred in many nations that have "hate speech" laws.[35] In Poland, a Catholic magazine was fined $11,000 for inciting "contempt, hostility and malice" by comparing a woman's abortion to the medical experiments at Auschwitz. The Dutch politician Geert Wilders was temporarily barred from entering Britain as a "threat to public policy, public security or public health" because he made a movie that called the Koran a "fascist" book and described Islam as a violent religion. In France, Brigitte Bardot was convicted of publishing a letter to the interior minister stating that Muslims were ruining France. Canada's human rights tribunal has targeted and harassed magazines for publishing anti-Muslim statements and for republishing the famous Danish Muhammad cartoons.

Another concern with "hate speech" laws is that they will be "enforced to stifle speech of the vulnerable, marginalized minority groups they are designed to protect."[36] In fact, this has been the case with regard to enforcement of "hate speech" laws in several developed democracies. It has also been true on American college campuses, where white students have invoked campus "speech codes" in response to speech by African American classmates. Atheists and agnostics might also be punished for violating "hate speech" laws. So might women participating in the #MeToo movement, who could be held liable for speech that denigrates men. Because

"hate speech" provisions can be used to further entrench racism and big-
otry, many minority speakers and groups oppose them.[37]

Finally, consider the very real possibility that powerful political factions
might use "hate speech" laws to suppress speech that criticizes government. A government empowered to suppress speech on the ground that it
communicates "hate" can also target its own critics. For example, the speech
of Black Lives Matter and other social justice critics might be suppressed on
the ground that it communicates hatred toward white people or the police.
"Hate speech" laws can thus be used to stifle even political dissent and criticism of government.

Much more can and indeed has been said concerning the complex
implications of "hate speech" laws. My goal is to both acknowledge the
harms associated with hateful and derogatory expression and to explain the
basic First Amendment doctrines and principles under which this expression remains mostly protected.

The United States is not likely to abandon its exceptional protection for
hateful speech. Thus, its people will have to continue to grapple with the
free speech, liberty, and equality implications of this exceptionalism. In
dealing with "hate speech," we can both acknowledge the harmful effects of
hateful expression, including the toll it takes on our political communities,
and defend the First Amendment principles that mostly protect it. What
we should not do, and what the Trump administration has mostly done,
is to deny these harms or disparage those who are concerned about them
as "radicals" and "bureaucrats." This will only continue to embolden and
encourage Americans and others to incite racial and other forms of hatred.

So what can be done? In her book, Professor Strossen discusses and
recommends a variety of non-censorial approaches to "hate speech."[38] One
approach leverages core First Amendment functions of counter-speech
and dissent. President Trump's derogatory statements actually show how
counter-speech can help a political community deal with the effects of
hateful speech. Each of candidate and President Trump's statements concerning African Americans, Mexicans, Muslims, the disabled, women, and
others has been met with a chorus of public criticism. President Obama
often encouraged students and others to respond to racist and demeaning
speech by using their own voices to condemn it. Many have followed that
approach.

Public condemnation has not removed the sting and stigma associated
with the president's comments. So far, at least, it has not seemed to change

either his mind or his behavior. However, as Justice Brandeis suggested, by meeting "evil" counsels with good ones, speakers have communicated their disapproval, solidarity, and resolve. They have stepped forward to insist that America not return to past eras, when racist and xenophobic communications were accepted as a "normal" part of social and political discourse. Mass dissent from the president's statements has also opened a new dialogue about the harms associated with hateful expression and the degree to which public officials ought to be held responsible for causing or exacerbating them. Each new social media video of a racist or anti-Semitic exchange on the streets, in a grocery store, or in the lobby of an apartment building has brought a chorus of outrage and a measure of public shaming.

Shortly after the deadly events in Charlottesville, at white suprem-acist demonstrations around the nation protesters and dissenters far outnumbered event participants. But counterdemonstrations are not nec-essary. Sometimes simply ignoring the speaker communicating hateful messages is an effective form of dissent. Thus, for example, rather than con-front alt-right speakers and white supremacists invited to campus, student activists may want to simply ignore them. Not showing up to a scheduled event deprives the hateful speaker of the power a boisterous or even violent reaction confers.

Social media companies should take these counter-speech functions to heart. As this book goes to print, Facebook, Twitter, and other sites are pla-nning to ban certain speakers from their platforms based on the deroga-tory content they have posted in the past. Since the First Amendment does not apply to these private decision-makers, they can take the censorial ap-proach. However, as several studies have shown, with respect to this con-tent the internet allows for very effective counter-speech and dissent.[39] The studies indicate that videos, satire, and other forms of counter-speech can be effective responses to derogatory content. On social media as elsewhere, counter-speech is often more effective at combatting "hate speech" than censorship and suppression.

Of course, "hate speech" is both a form of dissent and a means of suppressing the dissent of minorities. As discussed, one of the effects of some derogatory speech is to intimidate its targets into silence and submis-sion. As Strossen observes, effective counter-speech depends on the em-powerment of targeted audiences.[40] This, in turn, requires a commitment to educating, counseling, and training students and others to engage ef-fectively with "hate speech." Minorities and other targets of "hate speech" should not bear the entire burden of responding to hateful and derogatory expression. Members of a society who are truly committed to equality and individual dignity ought to condemn such speech and reject its premises. Those opposed to censorship ought to lead the way.

As Professor Strossen also observes, education can be a very effective form of counter-speech.[41] Education can entail everything from conveying accurate depictions of minorities in schools, media (including social media), and entertainment. We must also teach targets of hateful rhetoric to resist (to the extent practicable) and process such expression. At the same time, when it comes to the use of racist and other derogatory language, we ought to focus on instilling values such as self-restraint and empathy. As discussed in further detail later, government can play a positive, affirming, and non-coercive role in all of these respects.

In sum, we should neither deny the harms that "hate speech" can cause nor address them through censorship and suppression. The First Amendment may generally permit individuals and public officials to communicate hateful perspectives and opinions. However, the people are not powerless to resist this kind of expression. Indeed, as history and recent experience both indicate, counter-speech and dissent are among the most effective, but by no means exclusive, means of responding to demeaning and derogatory expression.

The Special Problem of Governmental Hate Speech

At various points in the book, I have drawn a distinction between governmental regulation of speech and the government's own speech. When he speaks in his official capacity, the president's opinions about race, religion, immigration, and other matters constitute government speech. When he communicates his own views on such matters, outside the context of any official policymaking function, the president is arguably communicating in his capacity as private citizen.

Ordinarily, the communication of private viewpoints would not raise concerns about the violation of others' First Amendment rights, since such statements carry no official weight or sanction. However, as the lawsuit concerning access to the president's Twitter page (discussed in chapter 4) demonstrates, it can be difficult to separate the president's official and private communications. When they issue from the mouth or social media account of the president, hateful and derogatory statements raise important and recurring concerns about the implications of governmental "hate speech." This is another aspect of the "hate speech" debate that merits special consideration in the Trump Era.

The Supreme Court has made clear that when the government itself or particular officials speak, the First Amendment does not limit what they can say.[42] This means that when it communicates, the government need not tolerate contrary viewpoints. If the people object to what they perceive to be hateful communications or statements by government officials, they are free to engage in counter-speech and dissent. However, their ultimate remedy is political rather than legal or constitutional. Thus, if voters object to the manner in which President Trump refers to racial and ethnic groups, or reject his policies on immigration and national security as bigoted, they have the ultimate power to vote him out of office.

There are some good reasons for allowing government to speak as it wishes on matters of public concern, free from concerns about content discrimination. In general, it is a positive thing for governments to be involved in debates on matters of public concern.[43] They add important perspectives and ideas to debates about economic policy, social justice, immigration, and other matters. Suppressing or constraining those perspectives would inhibit public discourse and exclude important perspectives.

However, throughout history, governments have also communicated racist, misogynist, and bigoted viewpoints. For example, segregationist laws communicated the inferiority of African Americans. These laws were fortified and supported by the "hate speech" of segregationist government officials. Segregationist *laws* were subject to challenge under the Equal Protection Clause of the Fourteenth Amendment and many were ultimately invalidated. However, during the civil rights era, the courts did not determine whether the government's own racist *communications* were themselves subject to any constitutional limits. Nor did they consider the specific constitutional injuries associated with laws and policies that express official views concerning racial inferiority.

President Trump's statements about white supremacists, Muslims, and women raise similar concerns. Suppose a government official like the president makes statements, either in his official capacity or in contexts in which the capacity is unclear, that denigrate Muslims or express contempt for individuals based on their race, ethnicity, or gender. Are those statements themselves subject to challenge under the Constitution?

The government's immunity as speaker is not absolute. For example, the Supreme Court has indicated that government speech is limited by the Establishment Clause of the First Amendment, which prohibits government from endorsing or denigrating particular religions.[44] The Establishment Clause requires that government maintain official neutrality concerning religion. It prohibits official policies or statements that single out particular religions for derogation. So when the president labels Muslims "terrorists," suggests that all mosques ought to be subject to government surveillance, or imposes a "travel ban" that targets Muslim refugees and immigrants, his statements at least implicate the Establishment Clause.[45]

To be clear, that does not mean that any Muslim offended by these statements could sue President Trump for violating her religious freedom. Among other things, the constitutional requirement that a person suffer a concrete injury and other complications associated with suing the president for constitutional violations, would prevent many suits like that from going forward. There are also questions about the legal and constitutional significance of derogatory presidential statements. In the litigation over the president's "Muslim ban" or "travel ban," the Supreme Court mildly rebuked President Trump for his statements about Muslims and Islam, but ultimately upheld the policy.[46] Although the president's statements were offensive and hurtful to Muslims, they ultimately had no legal or constitutional effect.

What about other constitutional rights? For example, do the equal protection rights guaranteed by the Fourteenth and Fifth Amendments impose any limits on governmental "hate speech"?[47] Some scholars think so, at least with respect to expressive *laws*. For instance, Professor Michael Dorf asks readers to consider a law requiring that all non-heterosexuals wear a visible pink triangle in public places.[48] The law compels the wearer to self-identify as non-heterosexual and communicates an "unmistakable message of second-class citizenship."[49] Although Professor Dorf notes that the harm from such a law is partly expressive,[50] the principal harm imposed by the hypothetical pink triangle law is subordination—the imposition of second-class status owing exclusively to a person's non-heterosexuality. That is a core concern of the equal protection guarantee, not the free speech provision. On this reasoning, laws and policies that communicate the second-class status of minorities implicate the equality rights of their targets, in part owing to the expressive effects of these measures.[51]

Professor Nelson Tebbe has argued that the harm in governmental "hate speech" is that it denies "full and equal citizenship" to targeted individuals.[52]

Professor Tebbe claims that this harm implicates equality, dignity, *and* free speech concerns. He notes that at least some free speech theorists would likely condemn racialized government speech, on the ground that it distorts democratic discourse.[53] Tebbe argues that racialized government speech "can constitute speakers as disregarded or disabled participants in political life."[54] He claims that this affects fundamental rights "to participation in the political community, including the freedom of expression."[55] Relatedly, as Professor Waldron has observed, hateful and derogatory expression can inhibit political participation—including dissent. It follows that official expression of this sort, which emanates from the highest levels of government, can inflict even greater damage on political discourse and political participation.

Constitutional scholars have raised important questions about the constitutional implications of hateful and derogatory communications by governmental speakers. We have not faced these concerns directly for six decades. President Trump's statements and policies about Muslims, women, the disabled, and others highlight concerns about the effect of governmental "hate speech" on religious, equality, free speech, and other rights. It is important that scholars continue to develop theories about the constitutional and other injuries associated with official "hate speech" and that litigants continue to bring these statements to the attention of courts.

However, at this moment, there are no judicially recognized limits on what we might call "pure" governmental "hate speech"—communications that denigrate or stir up hatred toward members of marginalized or politically powerless groups but are not connected to discriminatory laws or policies. The travel ban case shows that even when such laws or policies do exist, courts can ignore or downplay the hateful sentiments behind them.

Fortunately, there is another way of approaching the special problems of government speech as they pertain to concerns about equality and political citizenship. Although the present era makes the point somewhat difficult to appreciate, governments can make *positive* contributions to discourses about equality and citizenship. Political leaders can lead and educate the public on achieving equality, rather than divide them along racial, gender, and religious lines. Thus, rather than focus on the harms that government speech can produce, or the possibility of censoring official "hate speech," we might envision a different role for government. We might imagine government speech that is positive, uplifting, educational, and citizenship-affirming.

Scholars have imagined and indeed advocated on behalf of this more affirmative and benevolent form of government speaker.[56] For instance, the political scientist Corey Brettschneider has argued that the government should take affirmative steps to ensure that its citizens adopt liberal positions regarding free speech and equality. He thinks governments should do so not through coercive laws, but rather through means such as official communications, subsidy choices, the education of children, and other non-regulatory means.[57]

ProfessorBrettschneider's vision is based on a concept he calls "value democracy."[58] He argues that "a proper theory of freedom of expression also contains an essential role for the democratic state to publicize the reasons that underlie rights and legitimate law."[59] Thus, while he would extend free speech protection to hate groups and illiberal organizations that express discriminatory ideas, Brettschneider would also acknowledge the government's power to "defend the values of freedom and equality against discriminatory and racist challenges."[60] As he puts it, "The state should protect the rights of hate groups, while also criticizing their discriminatory views."[61]

During the Charlottesville "hate speech" controversy, President Trump's public remarks about "both sides" focused only on the first part of this formula. According to Professor Brettschneider, the government "has an obligation to clarify why some protected viewpoints are at odds with the reasons for free expression in the first place."[62] Thus, as it engages in "democratic persuasion," the government "has an obligation to explain why it respects viewpoint neutrality in the first place."[63] Without this dialogue, Brettschneider contends, "there is a significant risk that the real meaning of the protection of free expression will be inverted."[64] The public will walk away from incidents such as Charlottesville with the mistaken impression that the government supports the viewpoints being espoused, rather than understanding that they are protected in the hope that counter-speech and dissent will soundly defeat them.

Again, persuasion does not entail coercing citizens into believing in equality or respecting the dignity of others.[65] Brettschneider acknowledges that there should be "means-based" limits on government expression, including a prohibition on misleading, subliminal, and propagandizing communications.[66] He suggests that there could also be a "substance-based" limit, under which government is entitled to express itself only insofar as its communications facilitate ideals of free and equal citizenship.[67]

Within these limits, however, the government's power to persuade is potentially far-reaching. For instance, in order to facilitate racial equality, governments could persuade citizens to respect the equal citizenship of persons through direct communications, deny subsidies to groups that discriminate, and adopt school curricula that celebrate the contributions of civil rights leaders.[68]

These proposals may strike some as politically inappropriate and even inherently coercive. Note, however, that the "value democracy" approach does not seek to suppress or censor private "hate speech."[69] Rather, it attempts to leverage the government's voice to contextualize racist and other subordinating messages. It encourages governments, first and foremost, to *educate* their citizens as to why such speech must generally be tolerated. In this way, government speech can facilitate debates about the harms such speech entails and the normative reasons for respecting individual dignity and equality.

This positive approach to government speech offers a much-needed alternative to the negative, derogatory, and subordinating voice of our current era. As the Supreme Court observed in its decision upholding the Trump administration's travel ban, "The President of the United States possesses an extraordinary power to speak to his fellow citizens and on their behalf. Our Presidents have frequently used that power to espouse the principles of religious freedom and tolerance on which this Nation was founded."[70]

Presidents from Lincoln, to Kennedy, to Reagan, to Bush, to Obama have used official communications to uplift and affirm equality, religious, and other constitutional rights. One enduring lesson from this history is that government speech can be a source of affirmation rather than subordination. It can set a *positive* example for the body politic. One necessary corrective to the Trump Era is to return to this citizenship-affirming model of presidential communications.

6

Dissent

We must not confuse dissent with disloyalty. When the loyal opposition dies, I think the soul of America dies with it.[1]

As Professor Greg Magarian recently observed, "If a democracy doesn't make noise, it dies."[2] In a democracy, dissent is a particularly important type of "noise." As we have seen, the Trump Era has been characterized by a number of serious challenges to dissent and democratic discourse: persistent attacks on the press, demands for loyalty and the false equivalence of dissent and disloyalty, efforts to impose patriotic and other orthodoxies, limits on public access to public forums and public officials, and the amplification of "hate speech." This final chapter relates and connects these various challenges. It argues that together, they pose a serious threat to a precondition of American democracy—namely, the need to preserve a robust culture of dissent.

Dissent and the Trump Era

In order to understand why dissent is important to democracy, we must first understand the concept itself. At a basic level, dissent is the communication of disagreement. Think of it as the opposite of conformity.[3] Thus, for example, a protester who objects to a particular government policy disagrees—that is, dissents from—a policy that represents the status quo.

However, dissent is a much deeper and more nuanced concept than this simple example suggests. Professor Steven Shiffrin has offered three conceptions or definitions of dissent. He defines dissent as "speech that criticizes existing customs, habits, traditions, institutions, or authorities."[4] Shiffrin also defines dissent as the communication of "popularly disdained views."[5] Finally, Shiffrin characterizes dissent as "a social practice that

The First Amendment in the Trump Era. Timothy Zick.
© Timothy Zick 2019. Published 2019 by Oxford University Press.

challenges unjust hierarchies with the prospect of promoting progressive change."[6] One commentator has summarized Shiffrin's typology this way: "dissent as criticism of the status quo, dissent as the expression of unpopular views, and dissent as the promotion of progressive social change."[7]

The First Amendment protects all three forms of dissent. However, as Professor Cass Sunstein has observed, granting constitutional protection to dissent is not sufficient. We must also strive to preserve what he calls a "culture of dissent." As Sunstein writes:

> A well-functioning democracy has a *culture* of free speech, not simply legal *protection* of free speech. It encourages independence of mind. It imparts a willingness to challenge prevailing opinion through both words and deeds. Equally important, it encourages a certain set of attitudes in listeners, one that gives a respectful hearing to those who do not embrace the conventional wisdom. In a culture of free speech, the attitude of listeners is no less important than that of speakers.[8]

Professor Sunstein adds two important points about the concept of dissent. First, although it is necessary to do so, it is not enough to protect against official forms of censorship and suppression. Indeed, many of the Trump Era challenges to dissent do not stem from laws and regulations, but rather from the manner in which officials and citizens engage with and react to dissent and dissenters. Second, as Professor Sunstein observes, a *culture* of dissent does not merely tolerate criticism, but actively values, encourages, and facilitates it.

The previous chapters have examined restrictions on all three versions or types of dissent described by Professor Shiffrin—objection to the status quo, communication of unpopular views, and expression aimed at producing political and cultural change. Moreover, they have highlighted considerable obstacles to preserving a culture of dissent.

As discussed in chapter 1, a free and independent press publishes diverse content, ensuring that individuals have access to information that is necessary for self-government and the pursuit of truth. Although they have always been flawed institutions, the media remain the best source of information for "intelligent dissent."[9] Institutional media also act as watchdogs in terms of governmental abuse. Attempts to intimidate, discredit, and retaliate against individual reporters and media outlets constitute frontal attacks on the culture of dissent.

Chapter 2 showed that whatever form it takes, the concept of "sedition" threatens a vitally important check on official abuses of power. So do attempts to mandate or coerce loyalty to an office or officer, and to silence public employees who may have credible inside information about how government functions. As Madison wrote in the Virginia Resolution, such efforts ought to produce "universal alarm" because they undermine the "right of freely examining public characters and measures." As discussed later, they also lead to bad information cascades and decision-making—including voting—that is not supported by complete or accurate information.

Chapter 3 examined efforts to impose official or majoritarian orthodoxies with respect to patriotism, religion, and other matters of individual conscience. Nothing could be more inconsistent with the concept of dissent or the preservation of a culture of dissent. As Professor Shiffrin has observed with regard specifically to the punishment of flag-burning:

> If a central insight of First Amendment theory is that dissent deserves special protection, it follows that the state should not be able to punish flag burners. If America stands for free speech and free speech stands for dissent, the flag stands for dissent. To punish flag burners, from this perspective, contradicts the meaning of America.[10]

Chapter 4's discussion of the "public forum"—government properties that are open to expressive activity—showed that preserving "breathing space" for dissent helps to preserve a culture of dissent. Public forums are associated with a number of democratic and social functions of dissent, which are discussed in more detail later. For instance, access to the public forum "increas[es] the likelihood that dissenters will be able to confront those who might otherwise be blind conformists or fall into unjustified [information] cascades."[11] Access to streets, parks, and other public properties facilitates access to heterogeneous audiences and to specific audiences that influence policy outcomes (including presidents, members of Congress, and state officials). Public forums are especially important to dissenters, in particular because audiences cannot readily tune them out or avoid what they have to say. Further, in the digital era, new kinds of public forums, including governmental websites and official social media pages, will serve similar purposes. Denying access to these spaces will further undermine a culture of dissent.

Chapter 5's discussion of "hate speech" examined a complicated application of the principle of dissent and a contested aspect of the culture of dissent. Many view hateful and derogatory speech directed at racial, ethnic, and other minorities as unworthy not just of First Amendment protection but of the nation's culture of dissent. "Hate speech" can create a culture or climate of fear and intimidation, which in turn can chill dissent—particularly by minority speakers. However, maintaining a culture of dissent requires that we resist calls for censorship and allow the communication of opinions and ideas even if they are misguided, wrong, or motivated by hatred. A culture of dissent relies on counter-speech and other means of non-censorial dissent to defeat the forces of hate and division. As discussed, governments can play an important role not only by liberating dissent, but also by actively participating in discussions about hate, free speech, and equality. A culture of dissent can and should make room for public education about the rights and responsibilities of dissent.

As the various historical examples discussed in the book have shown, dissent has been a critical part of American constitutional, political, and cultural histories. In the Trump Era, Americans are again being called upon to remember and internalize the lessons, traditions, and values of dissent. History demonstrates that the experiment of American democracy cannot be successful without independent and analytical reporting, tolerance for criticism of political officials, resistance to official orthodoxies and tyrannical majorities (and politically connected minorities), breathing space for public protests, and the protection of viewpoints concerning matters of race, ethnicity, gender, and religion.

Dissent informs and educates citizens. It empowers them to resist authoritarianism and avoid blind fealty to political parties and individual politicians. In the current era, deep political and digital polarization is the new normal, intolerance for opposing political viewpoints seems to be at an all-time high, and truth itself is being re-characterized as simply a matter of one's personal beliefs. Preserving a culture of dissent is one of the principal challenges Americans now face.

Dissent and Democracy

The challenges of nurturing dissent and preserving a culture of dissent are not new. Our culture of dissent originated in the revolutionary period and was cemented during the founding. Having witnessed a revolution birthed in dissent, the Founders were acutely aware of the need for a free and independent press to check governmental abuses and, more generally, of the power of dissent to facilitate political mobilization and governmental reform.

That is not to say that subsequent generations of Americans always internalized and lived the lessons of revolutionary dissent. Indeed, particularly during wartime and times of global turmoil, the opposite has generally been true: dissent has been censored and dissenters severely punished. As discussed in chapter 2, the First Congress passed a Sedition Act and President Adams signed and vigorously enforced it against critics of himself and the war he was executing. During World War I, Congress enacted a second Sedition Act and vigorously pursued and prosecuted antiwar dissidents. During other periods, including the Cold War and the Vietnam War, dissenters were again persecuted, physically assaulted by fellow citizens, and jailed.

Over time, the Supreme Court began to recognize the importance to democracy of preserving and protecting dissent. In one of the most frequently quoted First Amendment opinions, Justice Brandeis wrote in *Whitney v. California*: "Those who won our independence by revolution were not cowards. They did not fear political change. They did not exalt order at the cost of liberty."[12] To the contrary, Brandeis observed:

> Those who won our independence believed that the final end of the State was to make men free to develop their own faculties; and that in its government the deliberative forces should prevail over the arbitrary. They valued liberty both as an end and as a means. They believed liberty to be the secret of happiness and courage to be the secret of liberty. They believed that freedom to think as you will and to speak as you think are means indispensable to the discovery and spread of political truth; that without free speech and assembly discussion would be futile; that with them, discussion affords ordinarily adequate protection against the dissemination of noxious doctrine; that the greatest menace to freedom is an inert people; that public discussion is a political duty; and that this should be a fundamental principle of the American government.[13]

The revolutionary experience Brandeis referred to was punctuated by an extraordinary degree of public dissent. As one scholar of the revolutionary period has observed, long before Americans had a recognized constitutional right to do so, colonists engaged "in every possible means of dissent available to them, from newspapers and pamphlets to songs, sermons, speeches, poems, plays, letters, petitions, liberty trees, and much more."[14] They were not always polite or subtle in demonstrating displeasure with the status quo. Indeed, public expression "could be erudite and even scholarly, but scurrilous often seemed more the norm."[15]

Nevertheless, not even serious concerns about "seditious libel" prosecutions were enough to deter speakers from debating the ratification of the Constitution, again often in caustic and critical terms. These robust debates influenced ratification of the First Amendment. As Justice Brandeis observed in *Whitney*, public dissent was considered not a fringe activity of "radicals" and "subversives" but a civic duty. Similarly, as James Madison observed in the Virginia Resolutions, dissent was part of the "right of freely examining public characters and measures, and of free communication among the people thereon, which has ever been justly deemed the only effectual guardian of every other right."[16]

The government's inclination to suppress dissent by ferreting out and punishing its critics is a key reason that free speech and press protections extend to those who challenge public officialdom. As discussed in chapter 1, the Supreme Court recognized in *N.Y. Times Co. v. Sullivan* that the First Amendment protects even "vehement, caustic, and sometimes unpleasantly sharp attacks on government and public officials." Indeed, as the Court observed, the "central meaning of the First Amendment" is that political dissent must be protected.

As Justice Brandeis's *Whitney* opinion also suggested, freedom to dissent nourished American democracy by opening space for public discourse and giving voice to the powerless and marginalized. Professor Shiffrin has observed:

> Dissent . . . is a practice of vital importance to the self-realization of many individuals, and even more important, a crucial institution for challenging unjust hierarchies and for promoting progressive change. It is also an important part of our national identity that we protect dissent.[17]

As noted, both the revolutionary and founding generations relied on a variety of means of expression to communicate opposition to government policies and criticism of public officials. Noisy and sometimes disruptive public demonstrations were some of the earliest manifestations of the First Amendment's power to effectuate political and social change. Dissenters also relied on symbolic forms of expression, including burning officials in effigy. Contrary to President Trump's view, these protests and other activities were not considered "embarrassing" to the nation. To the contrary, they were essential to its founding.

In terms of progressive change, the First Amendment's protections for dissent have facilitated social and constitutional movements from the American Revolution, to the abolition of slavery, to women's suffrage, to the civil rights movement, to today's movement on behalf of LGBT equality. As these and many other examples show, and as discussed in chapter 4, it is vitally important to create and preserve open public spaces—including, now, social media platforms—for the purpose of contention, argument, and dissent.[18] Characterizing assembled protesters as a form of "mob rule" again bespeaks a lack of knowledge and appreciation for a critically important part of American constitutional and political history.

History shows that democracies and democratic leaders prosper when they provide protection for dissent and invite candor and openness. By contrast, conformity, including to official orthodoxies and political tribes, leads to repression and extremism. As Professor Sunstein has observed: "Institutions are far more likely to succeed if they subject leaders to critical scrutiny and if they ensure that courses of action will face continuing monitoring and review from outsiders—if, in short, they use diversity and dissent to reduce the risks of error that come from social influences."[19] On this understanding of dissent, "I alone can fix it," as candidate Trump was fond of saying, is hardly a recipe for democratic success.

The right to dissent emboldens and empowers individuals to resist official orthodoxies and what John Stuart Mill called "the tyranny of the majority"—societal and political pressures to conform thoughts, beliefs, and actions. It protects the faculty member who refuses to sign a loyalty oath and the FBI director who balks at pledging personal loyalty—even to a president. The right to dissent gives athletes the fortitude to kneel when others insist that they stand. It instills a level of confidence in the flag-burner who desecrates what so many others hold to be sacred.

During the Trump Era, dissent has once again become a dirty word and disfavored practice. It has been unmoored from its revolutionary, constitutional, and democratic traditions by officials who either do not understand this history or who understand it but seek to chart a new path based on conformity and orthodoxy. Preserving a culture of dissent requires that the public and public officials embrace the democratic roots and benefits of criticism and nonconformity.

The Social Benefits of Dissent

In addition to its democratic benefits, dissent also serves a number of social functions. In the Trump Era, the characterization of dissenters as selfish rabble-rousers or participants in "mob rule" ignores the various communal benefits associated with dissent.

Dissenters challenge conventional wisdom, which is often mistaken and sometimes even dangerous. As Professor Sunstein has observed, even a lone dissenter can prevent or discourage false, unjustified, or harmful "information cascades"—a negative effect associated with conformity and groupthink.[20] By pointing out inconsistencies and exposing lies and mischaracterizations, dissenters contribute to more accurate decision-making.

As Professor Sunstein has also noted, dissent can help counteract the detrimental effects of group polarization.[21] As he explains, "like-minded people, after discussions with their peers, tend to end up thinking a more extreme version of what they thought before they started to talk."[22] Thus, because they are not confronted with opposing points of view, homogenous groups tend to take more extreme positions.

During the Trump Era, this has become an acute and growing problem. Partisan loyalties, widespread distribution of misinformation, and social media echo chambers have become common. Dissent can help counteract the polarizing effects of conformity, including increased levels of group outrage and political extremism. Within enclaves of like-minded people, members are likely to attribute evil motives to those outside the group. Such groups are also more likely to reject any form of compromise. In such environments, the orthodoxy of "political correctness" and the embrace of xenophobia are more likely to thrive.[23] Dissenters bring information and perspectives to these environments that may prevent or at least diminish outrage, extremism, and other effects of polarization.

Facilitating dissent also helps to amplify the voices of marginalized speakers and communities. In line with the informational advantages associated with information cascades and group polarization, society benefits from the distribution of information about minority views and preferences. As the Trump Era has demonstrated, dissent can generate substantive discussions about matters of vital public concern in this regard, including nationalism, social justice, racism, and religion. The proliferation of "hate speech" complicates this process, particularly if this form of dissent chills minority voices. However, as explained later on in this chapter, dissent from "hate speech" can also produce some valuable social benefits.

Finally, in terms of social benefits, dissent counteracts the increasingly atomistic character of our modern society. In the current era, we are increasingly ensconced in cultural, political, and digital bubbles. As Professor Shiffrin has observed, dissent fosters "engaged association" rather than atomistic individualism, because "[d]issenters seek converts and colleagues."[24] Thus, dissenters try to entice individuals to leave the comfort of their bubbles and to engage with different ideas and perspectives. Particularly in the digital era, which reinforces separatist and atomistic behavior, dissent can be helpful in terms of drawing people out into the open.

Thus, it is critically important that *societies* protect the activities of dissenters. Dissenters demonstrate courage in the face of calls for conformity. They set a positive example for others to come forward to challenge misinformation, bad decisions, and potentially false assumptions. They counteract the negative effects of widespread conformity. As Professor Sunstein notes, "conformists are free-riders."[25] Dissenters, by contrast, confer a number of benefits on fellow society members.

To be clear, these democratic and social values exist independent of any claim that dissenters are actually "right" or "right-thinking" people. Indeed, dissenters may be wrong or perhaps even dangerous. As Professor Sunstein observes, although there is a long "honor roll" of famous dissenters, there is a "dishonor roll" too, which includes Hitler, Lenin, and defenders of American slavery.[26] Thus, in addition to recognizing its benefits, we must be aware of the potential costs associated with dissent.

However, part of the reason we know who belongs on the "dishonor roll" is that the First Amendment protected not only their right to propose ideas but the public's right to resist and denounce them. The fact that dissenters can lead us in the wrong direction should not be viewed as grounds for suppressing their views. The argument for protecting dissent is not premised on some objective notion of truth. Rather, it is premised on dissent's role in the *pursuit* of more abstract notions of truth. This is why the First Amendment recognizes that false dissent—opinions held in error—can be just as valuable to that pursuit as is dissent based on objectively verifiable facts. As the political philosopher John Stuart Mill observed, false dissent can lead to "the clearer perception and livelier impression of truth, produced by its collision with error."[27]

As discussed in chapter 5, as applied to some forms of "hate speech" this argument is complex and controversial. After all, in this context there are "dissenters" on both sides—for example, proponents of equal justice and proponents of racial superiority. In some instances, protecting the communication of derogatory and hateful expression could suppress or discourage the speech of racial and other minorities. However, the First Amendment teaches that a public confrontation with racist views sharpens arguments and disagreements, prevents individuals from clinging to views out of mere prejudice, and deepens our understanding of equality. In this way, "hate speech" and the public response to it are also antidotes to things such as bad information cascades and group polarization.

Campus and other speech codes that purport to define which speech is too disdainful to be communicated raise the specter of enforced orthodoxy and pathological state control over public discourse. As discussed in chapter 5, public reaction to President Trump's statements concerning the Charlottesville, Virginia, demonstration showed that the public is capable of uniting to condemn and refute the concept of white supremacy. Hateful and derogatory dissent is protected not because, as Attorney General Sessions has suggested, suppressing it capitulates to "snowflakes" incapable of withstanding its serious harms. Rather, like other forms of dissent, "hate speech" is protected in part because it facilitates public discourse relating to equality, social justice and the pursuit of truth. As chapter 5 observed, it is also protected owing to concerns that governmental suppression will chill or censor the dissenting views of minority groups.

Over-Managing Dissent

Democracy and free expression thrive where there is noise and disagreement, not conformity and consensus. So far, the Trump Era has been characterized by an abundance of loud noise. However, the noise that matters most to democracy comes not from leaders but from the people. If the people are to remain vocal, they will need to make sure that public discourse and dissent are not over-managed.

Proposals to regulate, restrict, threaten, derogate, and prosecute dissenters are all worrisome evidence that the American tradition of dissent is once again under attack. However, in order to contextualize the current era, we must have an honest reckoning with our past.

But for the very notable exception of the American Revolution, most of the historical evidence points to a decided preference for conformity and order over dissent and disruption.[28] As Professor Geoffrey Stone and other scholars have shown, this is particularly true during wartime.[29] But it has been true during peacetime as well, as in the current era. Although our national narrative trumpets rambunctious and freewheeling dissent, the historical record suggests otherwise.

President Trump has successfully exploited a part of the American psyche that is comfortable with only certain kinds of criticism, protest, and dissent. His "law and order" mantra has resonated with a long-standing American counter-narrative, one that characterizes dissent as unruly and dangerous and that treats public displays of contention as evidence of "mob rule."

The lore of the First Amendment is that it protects vocal, offensive, and disruptive forms of dissent. To be sure, this perspective is reflected in the language of Supreme Court decisions. In *Terminiello v. City of Chicago*, for example, the Court wrote that speech "may indeed best serve its high purpose when it induces a condition of unrest, creates dissatisfaction with conditions as they are, or even stirs people to anger."[30] It went on to observe that "[s]peech is often provocative and challenging. It may strike at prejudices and preconceptions and have profound unsettling effects as it presses for acceptance of an idea."[31] In *New York Times Co. v. Sullivan*, the Supreme Court similarly wrote that debate on public matters should be "uninhibited, robust, and wide-open."[32]

However, a more conservative perspective with regard to public expression has often prevailed in the Court's First Amendment jurisprudence and in American society. Dissent that induces unrest, stirs people to anger, or creates dissatisfaction with the status quo has not actually received the favored or celebrated status suggested by the rhetoric in cases such as *Terminiello* and *Sullivan*. In fact, American First Amendment jurisprudence has long exhibited a preference for tamer and safer forms of dissent. That preference is reflected in how dissent, including criticism of officials and public protest, is currently being managed in American law and culture.

Despite the obvious importance of protecting dissent in times of war and global conflict, the Supreme Court's World War I–era free speech cases consistently upheld lengthy prison terms for speakers who did no more than distribute political pamphlets or make political speeches.[33] These speakers, the Court held, posed a "clear and present danger" to the war effort and to American society more generally. Even Justice Holmes's now-famous dissenting opinions from this era, which hinted at broader protection for free speech and press rights, consistently downplayed the danger these dissenters posed. He referred to them as "puny anonymities" who sought to communicate "silly" ideas.[34] Holmes did not offer any full-throated defense of dissent. In contrast, his characterizations suggested that the speech and speakers most worthy of First Amendment coverage and protection, or most entitled to it, were those that posed the least threat to social stability and political order.

Even in early peacetime decisions that upheld the right to speak in public places, the Supreme Court was willing to protect public dissent only to the extent that it did not actually stir anyone to anger or pose any threat to public order. Thus, in one case the Court overturned a breach of peace conviction against a Jehovah's Witness in part because he was "upon a public street, where he had a right to be, and where he had a right peacefully to impart his views to others."[35] There was no evidence, the Court observed, that the speaker's "deportment was noisy, truculent, overbearing or offensive."[36] He demonstrated no "intentional discourtesy."[37] Nor did the speaker intend to "insult or affront" his audience.[38] In another early case, the Court observed that epithets and swear words ("fighting words") directed at a person "without a disarming smile" were not entitled to any coverage under the Free Speech Clause.[39] In that case, the speaker, a Jehovah's Witness who had just been assaulted by a crowd, had referred to a public official as a "damn Fascist" and "a God damned racketeer."[40] The Court held that this form of dissent was not protected speech.

To be sure, these decisions were critically important victories for public expression. They established, for example, that speakers had a right to use the public sidewalks and streets to communicate with public audiences. However, they also clearly and consistently indicated that public dissent was likely to be protected by the Free Speech Clause only if it did not pose any serious challenge to social order, cause any actual disruption, or threaten the status quo—in other words, so long as it did not produce the results that dissent seeks to bring about.

This conception of carefully managed dissent continued even into the middle of the twentieth century. In *Feiner v. New York*,[41] the Court upheld the disorderly conduct conviction of a speaker who called political figures, including President Truman, "bums" and suggested that African Americans should "rise up" and fight for their equality rights.[42] Feiner was arrested owing to the reaction of a few onlookers, some of whom were apparently agitated by his speech (which of course was the point). According to the record in the case, his remarks "stirred up a little excitement."[43] One of the onlookers told police officers on the scene: "If you don't get that son of a bitch off, I will go over and get him off there myself."[44] Instead of arresting the onlooker, the police arrested Feiner—for his refusal to stop speaking when ordered to do so. The Court upheld the conviction, citing the city's overriding interest in "peace and order on its streets."[45]

Managed dissent was also the norm during the civil rights era, which many view as the heyday of freedom of expression and public protest on behalf of social justice. Civil rights protesters won important First Amendment victories relating to public dissent. However, the movement was committed to *peaceful* methods of protest. The violence and disruption typically originated with public officials and private parties, who were vehemently opposed to equal rights for African Americans. In some post-*Feiner* civil rights cases, the Court invalidated breach of peace convictions on what seemed like very similar facts. But it again emphasized that those who had assembled were engaged in passive demonstrations and peaceful marches.[46]

Other decisions handed down during the civil rights era adopted a similar perspective concerning dissenters' rights. For example, the Supreme Court held that civil rights protesters had a free speech right to engage in a *silent* protest in a public library reading room—although, as reflected in the various opinions, protecting even this form of dissent divided the Court.[47] It was clear that if the protesters had done anything other than merely sit or stand—if they had spoken in non-hushed tones, or moved about the library reading room, or displayed a "truculent bearing"—the result would have been different. During the Vietnam War Era, the Court similarly held that public elementary and junior high school students could wear black armbands in *silent* protest of the Vietnam War—that is, so long as their speech did not "materially disrupt studies or invade the rights of others."[48]

By contrast, when civil rights protesters got too close for comfort to government buildings such as schools and jailhouses, the Court did not hesitate to uphold their breach of peace and disorderly conduct convictions.[49] Moreover, the Court saw no merit in First Amendment challenges to segregation in public accommodations such as lunch counters.[50]

This is not to say that the Supreme Court failed to recognize, and indeed in some instances even expanded upon, First Amendment rights to communicate public dissent and to criticize government. The Court refashioned tort law to permit speakers to engage in robust and sometimes caustic criticism of government and public figures.[51] It also defended offensive forms of dissent. In *Cohen v. California*, for example, the Court overturned the conviction of a man who wore a jacket emblazoned with the words "Fuck the Draft" into the corridor of a public courthouse—in part, it bears noting, because no one in the corridor was stirred to anger or disturbed by the jacket.[52] And, as noted, the Court upheld the right to dissent in public streets and other places—again, so long as the display did not result in any violent reaction or disruption of government functions.

Even *Brandenburg v. Ohio*,[53] a celebrated decision that narrowed the standard for "incitement" to unlawful action and thereby created invaluable breathing space for political dissent, involved the sort of "puny anonymities" Justice Holmes referred to in his early dissent. In *Brandenburg*, a group of KKK members had burned some crosses in a rural Ohio field and communicated racist and anti-Semitic messages to those in attendance.[54] They engaged in some tall talk—that is, taking "revengeance" against the government.[55] But like other public speakers who prevailed in First Amendment challenges, this group, despite its deplorable rhetoric, was orderly, non-disruptive, and decidedly non-threatening. To convey their grievances, they called for a peaceful march to Washington, DC, and perhaps other places.

In sum, despite the liberalization of the *right* to dissent, many First Amendment precedents have not embraced a culture of dissent that included speech that "created conditions of unrest" or "stirred people to anger."[56] Indeed, in some respects, the American free speech narrative of "uninhibited and wide-open discourse" has actually been more myth than reality. As interpreted, the First Amendment has largely protected speakers who tow a certain line in terms of accepted social and political behavior. Silent protests and expressive activities that did not upset social norms and sensibilities were generally treated as protected speech. However, burning a draft card as part of an otherwise peaceful public protest, protesting next to a jail where alleged political prisoners were being held, uttering "dirty words" on the radio as part of a political commentary about censorship, or sleeping overnight in a park near the U.S. Capitol have not been granted

First Amendment protection.[57] The Court considered these forms of dissent a bit too "robust, uninhibited, or wide-open."

The preference for peaceful, orderly, and non-disruptive dissent is generally consistent with the manner in which dissent—particularly public demonstrations and displays—has been managed. As discussed in chapter 4, the "public forum" doctrine narrowly circumscribes the places that are open to collective and other forms of expression.[58] Pursuant to that doctrine, dissenters have a right of access to public streets, parks, and other properties that have traditionally been open to expressive uses. But other public properties are not presumptively open to expressive activities, and government retains broad authority to preserve them for other intended uses.[59] With regard to *private* property, the First Amendment does not require owners to provide dissenters with any access at all.[60]

As discussed, in order to maintain safety, order, tranquility, and even aesthetic appeal, governments are generally authorized to impose "time, place, and manner" regulations in public forums so long as they do not target the content of expression. Thus, the places where speakers are permitted to dissent, the manner in which they can do so, and the times when dissent is permitted all generally fall under the government's broad managerial authority.[61]

In the Trump Era, as in the past, detailed permit requirements, which include restrictions that affect various aspects of public dissent, are a common feature of public forum management. Even small groups seeking to stage a demonstration or protest must sometimes navigate a gauntlet of permit regulations, advance notice requirements, fees, route restrictions, time and size limits, and conduct proscriptions. In addition, as described in chapter 4, First Amendment doctrines generally allow, if not encourage, government to control dissent through a variety of spatial and other tactics.[62]

To be sure, modern First Amendment doctrines prohibit the kind of unbridled discretion officials used to exercise with regard to public dissent. However, they have been roundly criticized for imposing a rigid managerial regime that diminishes opportunities to dissent.[63] Even in places where dissenters ostensibly have First Amendment rights, detailed regulations are used to manage and control dissent and other forms of expression. As chapter 4 emphasized, the gradual loss of public space and the strict management of public places under the government's control—including through the implementation of "command and control" and other aggressive policing methods—often disparately affect those who wish to communicate dissenting viewpoints. States and localities continue to propose new limits on public protests and demonstrations. As they have recently, such proposals tend to increase after high-profile demonstrations.

In the current era, the United States continues to struggle with the balance between public contention and public order. "Law and order" policies, proposals to banish flag-burners and treat dissenters as disloyal subversives, and prosecutions for even minor shows of dissent (the woman who chuckled at the Sessions confirmation hearing comes to mind) are all part of a familiar historical pattern.

Some evidence suggests that a preference for strictly managed dissent is baked into the American psyche. Public opinion polling suggests that while they are generally supportive of freedom of speech, Americans remain ambivalent about certain forms of dissent. For example, in a recent poll, a majority responded that a person who burns the U.S. flag should lose his or her citizenship (not coincidentally, the very proposal floated by President Trump) and that controversial speakers should be banned from campus if students are likely to engage in violent protests in response to the speaker's presence.[64]

Americans have historically been wary of large-scale displays of dissent. As one organization that tracks public opinion regarding protest movements has observed, "the public's overall attitude regarding mass demonstrations seems to range from skepticism to outright condemnation."[65] These attitudes extend also to protest *movements*. Civil rights, antiwar, and economic justice movements have all received low levels of support from the American public. In sum, public opinion polling suggests that Americans prefer managed dissent to the kind that upsets, stirs to anger, or unsettles.

In important respects, our law, politics, and culture all actively discourage dissent. Preferences for order, conformity, and the status quo are built into our jurisprudence, architecture, policing, and public attitudes. As the Trump Era once again reminds us, these are individually and collectively significant obstacles to overcome if we are to preserve a culture of dissent.

Truth and Dissent

There are other serious warning signs for dissent and the culture of dissent. Even before Donald Trump's election, "truth" had become an increasingly elastic concept. During the Trump Era, an actual war on truth has broken out. In this era of "alternative facts," one presidential advisor actually asserted that "facts are not facts." And the president has himself proclaimed, to a public audience, that "what you're seeing and what you're reading is not what's happening."

Truth has a special relationship to dissent. In order to provide the democratic and social benefits discussed earlier, dissent requires some agreement on a baseline of objective facts, access to verifiably accurate information, and reliable information about the status quo. In order to object to the way things are, dissenters need accurate information about current and past conditions. If the government, which is often the source of such information, obscures the truth of these matters, makes up its own reality, or engages in outright falsehoods, effective dissent becomes difficult if not impossible. Interference by outside forces, including foreign adversaries, with the American truth-seeking process also undermines dissent and puts democracy in peril.

A government willing to engage in or even tolerate disinformation tactics is more difficult to hold accountable. If criticism can simply be dismissed as "fake news" and if "facts aren't facts," then the self-government and marketplace of ideas models that democracy relies upon cannot function properly. If critics can be dismissed as charlatans, partisans, or purveyors of "fake news," then group polarization, conformity, and bad information cascades will continue to proliferate.

The war on truth is part and parcel of the war on dissent. If partisans can simply make up their own truths, dissent is likely to become more and more marginalized. If dissent is defined as being in opposition to something— that is, the economic status quo or immigration policies—then we must have some basic agreement with regard to things such as employment figures and net migration patterns. If we cannot distinguish good information from bad, dissent cannot serve its democratic, social, and other functions.

Creating and Preserving a Culture of Dissent

As the book's chapters have emphasized, there are at present many serious challenges to protecting dissent and maintaining a culture of dissent in the United States: attacks on the independence and freedom of an already fragile press, the revival of the concept of "sedition," efforts to impose official orthodoxies regarding patriotism and other matters, restrictions on access to public forums, and the proliferation of "hate speech." In one sense, President Trump has done us the favor of openly challenging dissent and specific dissenters. His boasting of efforts to undermine dissent means we need not guess as to his motives or purposes. Still, we need to have a plan of attack to deal with this anti-dissent agenda and to preserve a culture of dissent moving forward.

Professor Shiffrin has helpfully sketched some of the critical elements of such a plan. Some of his suggestions have been discussed or hinted at in prior chapters. They include educating citizens about the values of dissent and the skills necessary to respond to rather than censor opposing viewpoints, preserving open channels of expression, minimizing legal and cultural barriers to dissent, and ensuring the free flow of information.[66]

We must also find some way to rescue the concept of "truth" from utter subjectivity by distinguishing it from notions such as "alternative facts" and personal "beliefs." In particular, we cannot allow government to determine or dictate what "truth" is with regard to politics, faith, or other matters.

A pro-dissent agenda must have the goal not merely of increasing *tolerance* for dissent, but rather looking toward its active facilitation and encouragement.[67] As discussed, however, we also have much work to do on the tolerance front. First Amendment jurisprudence sets the stage by preferring non-disruptive forms of dissent. Polling indicates that many Americans view certain forms of dissent as threatening to societal order and unworthy of protection. Court precedents and public attitudes pose serious obstacles to any agenda aimed at creating and sustaining a culture of dissent. That culture must make ample room for disruptive, noisy, and antagonistic expression.

At a minimum, people must feel free to speak out. In the current era, the pressure to conform is sometimes intense. In a hyper-partisan culture, people feel compelled to choose "sides." Dissenters fear being treated not as valued nonconformists, but rather as disloyal enemies.

In a recent radio interview, a Dearborn, Michigan, resident who was originally from Iraq reported that he felt compelled to support President Trump's travel ban and other immigration policies—owing to the fear that because he and his family are Muslim, neighbors would blame them for any future terrorist attack by an immigrant. This anecdote highlights the deep and complex undercurrents that contribute to a culture of conformity and suppress dissent. The president's practice of demonizing immigrants is problematic for many reasons—including its downstream effect on local dissent.

In some venues, people are vigorously engaging in dissent. Social media sites such as Facebook and Twitter contain a significant amount of dissent—much of it facilitated by the cloak of anonymity. As discussed in chapter 5, online dissent is a partial antidote to hateful and derogatory speech—which is itself a crude form of dissent.

Whether a culture of dissent can actually thrive on social media platforms depends a lot on how owners and managers of those spaces regulate speakers and expression in the future. Social media entities are now aware of the problem of manufactured content emanating from abroad—including "fake news" that has been distributed with the intention of manufacturing dissent and exacerbating political divisions. Taking measures to combat this aspect of the war on truth will be critically important to the future of the culture of dissent.

As they do in the physical world, blatant forms of censorship in cyberspace will undermine the culture of dissent. Platforms are currently struggling to balance human rights, constitutional rights, and expressive values. They have a tremendous—and to some, troubling—degree of influence over the nature of the culture of dissent. Social media policies and practices that ban speakers or remove content based on user complaints or algorithms will naturally affect dissent. In a global community, taking such actions may be necessary in order to comply with human or constitutional rights. However, social media entities must factor into the equation the extent to which their platforms will censor or quash dissent in the process.

User habits matter too. Even now, there is a lot of cyber-sorting and user siloing going on in cyber places. As discussed earlier, this leads to homogenous groups, information cascades, and group polarization. In this sense, social media imitate a social landscape in which participants self-segregate and polarize. If social media creates echo chambers, dissenters will not be heard.

Further, like their offline counterparts, online mobs and trolls can substantially undermine dissent. Indeed, the costs imposed by online mobs can be far more serious and long-term than those associated with shaming and other forms of retribution in tangible places.[68] Here, again, dissenters will need to develop the tools to respond to things such as online shaming and trolling, which pose serious challenges to the development of a healthy cyberculture of dissent. Law has some role to play here. Prohibiting online harassment and threatening speech can create a safer environment and some breathing space for nonconformists.

History shows that it will not be easy to facilitate dissent and nurture a culture of dissent. Education, including government speech that extolls the virtues of dissent rather than criticizes it as illegitimate or "embarrassing," would certainly help to create a friendlier climate for dissenters. However, in the Trump Era, that is obviously not where we find ourselves. Dissent and dissenters have been denigrated and devalued once more—this time, not in the service of some wartime agenda but primarily because they express views that are critical of the current administration.

A quick glance around the word, to events in places such as Brazil, Hungary, and Saudi Arabia, indicates where a culture of fear and the coordinated suppression of dissent can lead. Despite the anti-dissent agenda, the United States is not yet in this dire position. The First Amendment protects dissenters' rights. Even if they have not embraced disruptive dissent, courts stand firmly behind the broad principle of content-neutrality. Legally and constitutionally, the culture of dissent cannot be quashed by authoritarian rules or outright state suppression.

However, one of the critical lessons of the Trump Era is that leaders who do not value dissent, and what is more seek to quash it through retaliatory threats, can still significantly undermine the culture of dissent. The tone of a culture is set in large part by cultural and governmental leaders. One of the changes Trump has brought to the presidency is that he serves in both capacities. Future leaders may similarly straddle entertainment and governance in ways that likewise influence the culture of dissent. Their words and gestures will make a significant difference in terms of how much dissent is tolerated, facilitated, and practiced.

Professor Geoffrey Stone, who has written extensively about dissent, has offered his own prescription for preserving a culture of dissent in the United States. It is difficult to improve upon. Writing against the backdrop of governmental suppression of dissent during wartime, Professor Stone observed:

> To strike the right balance [between fear and freedom], this nation needs political leaders who know right from wrong; federal judges who will stand fast against the furies of their age; members of the bar and the academy who will help Americans see themselves clearly; a thoughtful and responsible press; informed and tolerant citizens who will value not only their

own liberties, but the liberties of others; and justices of the Supreme Court with the wisdom to know excess when they see it and the courage to preserve liberty when it is imperiled. And, so, we shall see.[69]

So, as President Trump is fond of saying, "we'll see what happens . . ." If history is any guide, the American people will continue to engage in acts of dissent and play their part in terms of checking authoritarian impulses. They cannot sustain the culture of dissent on their own. This can happen only through protection of the free and independent distribution of information by the press, preservation of ample breathing space for nonconformists and protesters, and the public recognition that without dissent democracy dies.

Notes

Introduction

1. Jenna Johnson & Mary Jordan, "Trump on Rally Protester: 'Maybe He Should Have Been Roughed Up,'" *Wash. Post* (Nov. 22, 2015), https://perma.cc/9632-GM49. A federal appeals court later absolved candidate Trump of civil liability for the physical assaults that occurred at one of his campaign rallies. See Nwanguma v. Trump, 903 F.3d 604 (6th Cir. 2018).
2. Michael M. Grynbaum, "Trump Renews Pledge to 'Take a Strong Look at Libel Laws,'" *N.Y. Times* (Jan. 10, 2018), B3.
3. Eli Rosenberg, "Trump Admitted He Attacks Press to Shield Himself from Negative Coverage," *Wash. Post* (May 22, 2018).
4. See "Americans' Views on the Media: Ipsos Poll Shows Almost a Third of the American People Agree That the News Media Is the Enemy," (Aug. 7, 2018) https://www.ipsos.com/en-us/news-polls/americans-views-media-2018-08-07.
5. See Marvin Kalb, *Enemy of the People: Trump's War on the Press, The New McCarthyism, and the Threat to American Democracy* (Brookings Institute Press, 2018).
6. N.Y. Times Co. v. Sullivan, 376 U.S. 254, 270 (1964).
7. West Va. State Bd. of Educ. v. Barnette, 319 U.S. 624 (1943).
8. Texas v. Johnson, 491 U.S. 397 (1989).
9. Keyishian v. Board of Regents, 385 U.S. 589 (1967).
10. Knight First Amendment Inst. at Columbia Univ. v. Trump, 302 F. Supp. 3d 541 (S.D.N.Y. 2018).
11. See generally Alexander Meiklejohn, *Free Speech and Its Relation to Self-Government* (Harper Bros., 1948); John Milton, *Areopagitica: A Speech for the Liberty of Unlicensed Printing* 45, ed. H.B. Cotterill (MacMillan 1959); Abrams v. United States, 250 U.S. 616, 630 (1919) (Holmes, J., dissenting) (observing that free speech facilitates a "marketplace in ideas"). See also C. Edwin Baker, *Human Liberty and Freedom of Speech* (Oxford Univ. Press, 1992).
12. See, e.g., Pleasant Grove City v. Summum, 555 U.S. 640, 647 (2009) ("[I]f the government is engaging in [its] own expressive conduct, then the Free Speech Clause has no application."). See also Walker v. Texas Division, Sons of Confederate Veterans, 135 S. Ct. 2239 (2015) (concluding that specialty state license plates are a form of government speech).
13. See Sonja R. West, "Suing the President for First Amendment Violations," 71 *Okla. L. Rev.* 321 (2018) (summarizing arguments against presidential liability and potential responses). Scholars taking this position include Daniel J. Hemel,

The First Amendment in the Trump Era. Timothy Zick.
© Timothy Zick 2019. Published 2019 by Oxford University Press.

"Executive Action and the First Amendment's First Word," 40 *Pepp. L. Rev.* 601, 601 (2013); Nicholas Quinn Rosenkrantz, "The Subjects of the Constitution," 62 *Stan. L. Rev.* 1209, 1250 (2010); Gary Lawson & Guy Seidman, *The Constitution of Empire: Territorial Expansion and American Legal History* 42–43 (Yale Univ. Press, 2004); Jay S. Bybee, "Common Ground: Robert Jackson, Antonin Scalia, and a Power Theory of the First Amendment," 75 *Tul. L. Rev.* 251, 326 (2000).

Chapter 1

1. Rosenbloom v. Metromedia, Inc., 403 U.S. 29, 51 (1971), abrogated by Gertz v. Robert Welch, Inc., 418 U.S. 323 (1974).
2. See Sonja R. West, "Presidential Attacks on the Press," 80 *Mo. L. Rev.* 915 (2018).
3. RonNell Anderson Jones & Sonja West, "The Fragility of the Free American Press," 112 *Nw. U. L. Rev. Online* 47, 49 (2017).
4. PEN America Center, Inc. v. Donald J. Trump, Civil Action No. 18-cv-9433-LGS (S.D.N.Y 2019).
5. Id., amended complaint at 1.
6. Id. at 2–3.
7. Id. at 1.
8. See New York Times Co. v. Sullivan, 376 U.S. 254, 270 (1964) (observing that free speech and press protections of the First Amendment "reflect a profound national commitment to the public principle that debate on public issues should be uninhibited, robust, and wide-open, and that it may well include vehement, caustic, and sometimes unpleasantly sharp attacks on government and public officials.").
9. David A. Anderson, "Freedom of the Press," 80 *Tex L. Rev.* 429, 430 (2002).
10. See, e.g., Eugene Volokh, "Freedom of the Press as an Industry, or for the Press as a Technology? From the Framing to Today," 160 *U. Penn. L. Rev.* 459, 538–39 (2012) (arguing that the Press Clause has been understood throughout American history to guarantee "equal treatment to [all] speakers without regard to whether they are members of the press-as-industry").
11. Id.
12. See *Sullivan*, 376 U.S. at 256 ("We are required in this case to determine for the first time the extent to which the constitutional protections for speech and press limit a State's power to award damages in a libel action brought by a public official against critics of his official conduct."). The Court used some version of the formulation "freedoms of speech and press" throughout its opinion. See, e.g., id. at 265.
13. See Melville Nimmer, "Introduction—Is Freedom of the Press a Redundancy: What Does It Add to Freedom of Speech?," 26 *Hastings L. J.* 639, 640 (1975). Not all scholars agree with that assessment. See, e.g., Jud Campbell, "Natural Rights and the First Amendment," 127 *Yale L. J.* 246 (2017) (concluding, based on natural law understandings, that freedom of speech and freedom of press comprised distinctive guarantees).

14. See, e.g., Branzburg v. Hayes, 408 U.S. 665, 704 (1972) (observing that defining the press for purposes of evidentiary privileges "would present practical and conceptual difficulties of a high order").

15. Some media representatives were wary of seeking special "press" rights for this reason. See RonNell Anderson Jones, "The Dangers of Press Clause Dicta," 48 *Ga. L. Rev.* 705, 718–19 (2014). As Sonja West has noted, "[t]he justices' understandable desire to avoid favoring an elite group has led them to allow the Speech Clause to swallow the Press Clause." West, supra note 2, at 1031.

16. Address by Mr. Justice Stewart, Yale Law School Sesquicentennial Convocation, November 2, 1974, reprinted in Stewart, "Or of the Press," 26 *Hastings L.J.* 631 (1975).

17. See generally Nimmer, supra note 13.

18. See West, supra note 2, at 1033–41. See also Randall P. Bezanson, "Whither Freedom of the Press?," 97 *Iowa L. Rev.* 1259, 1273 (2012) ("We need a guarantee of freedom of the press distinct from freedom of speech.").

19. See First Nat'l Bank v. Belotti, 435 U.S. 765, 799–800 (1978). See also David Lange, "The Speech and Press Clauses," 23 *UCLA L. Rev.* 77, 88 (1975) (interpreting the free speech and press provisions as interchangeable).

20. First National Bank v. Bellotti, 435 U.S. 765, 800 (1978) (Burger, J., concurring).

21. See Timothy Zick, *The Dynamic Free Speech Clause: Free Speech and Its Relation to Other Constitutional Rights* ch. 3 (Oxford Univ. Press, 2018) (discussing the treatment of speech, press, assembly, and petition as different aspects of a "free expression" right).

22. See C. Edwin Baker, "The Independent Significance of the Press Clause under Existing Law," 35 *Hofstra L. Rev.* 955, 956 (2007) ("The Court has never explicitly recognized that the Press Clause involves any significant content different from that provided to all individuals by the prohibition on abridging freedom of speech."). See also Richmond Newspapers, Inc. v. Virginia, 448 U.S. 555 (1980) (invalidating trial court closure order on grounds that public and press have a right to attend trial proceedings).

23. 4 W. Blackstone, *Commentaries on the Laws of England* 151–52 (Oxford, 1769).

24. See Leonard Levy, *Freedom of the Press from Zenger to Jefferson* lv–lvi (Bobbs-Merrill, 1966).

25. See Patterson v. Colorado, 205 U.S. 454 (1907) (suggesting that First Amendment protection was limited to invalidating prior restraints).

26. See Leonard Levy, *Legacy of Suppression: Freedom of Speech and Press in Early American History* 214–15 (Harvard Univ. Press, 1960) (observing that "freedom of the press was everywhere a grand topic for declamation").

27. See David A. Anderson, "The Origins of the Press Clause," 30 *UCLA L. Rev.* 455, 465 (1983) (observing that of the early state constitutions, only Pennsylvania's contained a free speech provision).

28. See Akhil Amar, *The Bill of Rights: Creation and Reconstruction* 20–26 (discussing free speech and free press); 26–32 (discussing assembly and petition) (Yale Univ. Press., 1998).

29. See generally Stephen D. Solomon, *Revolutionary Dissent: How the Founding Generation Created the Freedom of Speech* (St. Martin's Press, 2016).

30. 376 U.S. 254, 270 (1964).

31. Id. at 276.

32. Id. at 273.

33. Id.

34. Id. at 277–78.

35. E.g., Fla. Star v. B.J.F., 491 U.S. 524, 525 (1989); Hustler Mag., Inc. v. Falwell, 485 U.S. 46, 46-47 (1988).

36. Citizens United v. FEC, 558 U.S. 310, 352 (2010) ("We have consistently rejected the proposition that the institutional press has any constitutional privilege beyond that of other speakers.").

37. West, supra note 2, at 1069–70.

38. Branzburg v. Hayes, 408 U.S. 665, 702–03 (1972) .

39. Jones & West, supra note 3, at 54.

40. See Mary-Rose Papandrea, "Citizen Journalism and the Reporter's Privilege," 91 *Minn. L. Rev.* 515, 546 & nn.175, 176 (2007) (collecting citations to state laws recognizing qualified reporters' privilege).

41. Jones & West, supra note 3, at 55–63.

42. Id.

43. Id.

44. Lyrissa Barnett Lidsky, "Not a Free Press Court?," 2012 *BYU L. Rev.* 1819 (2012).

45. See Amy Gadja, *The First Amendment Bubble* 55–60 (Harv. Univ. Press, 2015).

46. RonNell Anderson Jones, "What the Supreme Court Thinks of the Press and Why It Matters," 66 *Ala. L. Rev.* 253, 255 (2014); RonNell Andersen Jones, "Justice Scalia and Fourth Estate Skepticism," 15 *First Amend. L. Rev.* 258, 264–65 (2017).

47. Jones, "What the Supreme Court Thinks," supra note 46, at 266-68.

48. Jones & West, supra note 3, at 59.

49. Id.

50. Id. at 60.

51. Id. at 61–62.

52. Id. at 49.

53. Minneapolis Star & Tribune Co. v. Minn. Comm'r of Revenue, 460 U.S. 575, 585 (1983) (alteration in original) (citation omitted) (quoting Grosjean v. Am. Press Co., 297 U.S. 233, 250 (1936)).

54. Cox Broadcasting Corp. v. Cohn, 420 U.S. 469, 491 (1975).

55. Id. at 492.

56. Estes v. Texas, 381 U.S. 532, 539 (1965).

57. Mills v. Alabama, 384 U.S. 214, 219 (1966).

58. Leathers v. Medlock, 499 U.S. 439, 447 (1991).

59. Minneapolis Star & Tribune Co. v. Minn. Comm'r of Revenue, 460 U.S. 575, 585 (1983).

60. *Mills*, 384 U.S. at 219.

61. New York Times Co. v. Sullivan, 376 U.S. 254, 275 (1964) (quoting 4 *Elliot's Debates on the Federal Constitution* 570 (1876)).

62. Jones, "What the Supreme Court Thinks," supra note 46, at 255–56.

63. See New York Times Co. v. United States, 403 U.S. 713 (1971) (invalidating judicial injunctions prohibiting publication of the Pentagon Papers); United States v. Nixon, 418 U.S. 683 (1974) (rejecting president's claim of "executive privilege" covering audiotapes relating to Watergate burglary and cover-up).

64. Time, Inc. v. Hill, 385 U.S. 374, 388–89 (1967) (quoting 4 Elliot's Debates, at 571).

65. Sheppard v. Maxwell, 384 U.S. 333, 350 (1966).

66. Id. (quoting Report on the Virginia Resolutions, Madison's Works, vol. iv, 544).

67. 283 U.S. 697, 718 (1931).

68. Id. at 719.

69. Solomon, supra note 29, at 297–98.

70. Thomas Jefferson to Monsieur A. Coray, 31 October 1823, in *The Writings of Thomas Jefferson*, ed. H.A. Washington ch. 7, 323–24 (Taylor & Murray, 1854).

71. E.g., Henry Monaghan, "Of 'Liberty' and 'Property,'" 62 *Cornell L. Rev.* 405 (1977); Richard Epstein, "Was *New York Times v. Sullivan* Wrong?," 53 *U. Chi. L. Rev.* 782 (1986).

72. E.g., David Anderson, "Libel and Press Self-Censorship," 53 *Tex. L. Rev.* 422 (1975).

73. New York Times Co. v. United States, 403 U.S. 713 (1971) (Douglas, J., concurring).

74. See Sherrill v. Knight, 569 F.2d 124, 129 (D.C. Cir. 1977) ("The protection afforded to newsgathering under the first amendment guarantee of freedom of the press requires that . . . access [to White House press facilities] not be denied arbitrarily or for less than compelling reasons.").

75. Solomon, supra note 29, at 297.

76. Id. at 279.

77. For a forward-looking agenda for a free and independent press, see Lee C. Bollinger, *Uninhibited, Robust, and Wide Open: A Free Press for a New Century* (Oxford Univ. Press, 2010).

78. See "Americans' Views on the Media: Ipsos Poll Shows Almost a Third of the American People Agree That the News Media Is the Enemy," https://www.ipsos.com/en-us/news-polls/americans-views-media-2018-08-07.

79. *The Records of the Federal Convention of 1787*, ed. Max Farrand, vol. 3, appendix A, p. 85 (1911, reprinted 1934).

Chapter 2

1. 4 Annals of Congress, p. 934 (1794) (James Madison).

2. New York Times Co. v. Sullivan, 376 U.S. 254, 270 (1964).

3. Elizabeth Goitein, "In a Crisis, the President Can Invoke Extraordinary Authority. What Might Donald Trump Do with This Power?", *The Atlantic* (Jan./Feb. 2019), at 39.

4. See Timothy Zick, *Speech Out of Doors: Preserving First Amendment Liberties in Public Places* (Cambridge Univ. Press, 2009). See also Ronald J. Krotoszynski Jr., *Reclaiming the Petition Clause: Seditious Libel, "Offensive" Protest, and the Right to Petition the Government for Redress of Grievances* (Yale Univ. Press, 2012).

5. Krotoszynski, supra note 4, at 7.

6. Alan M. Dershowitz, "Trump's Bid to Silence Dissent Violates Spirit of First Amendment," *Boston Globe*, (Jul. 25, 2018). (https://www.bostonglobe.com/opinion/2018/07/25/trump-bid-silence-dissent-violates-spirit-first-amendment/czPW9wyCBsSwkxIvvB5dvJ/story.html).

7. Brandenburg v. Ohio, 395 U.S. 444 (1969).

8. See, e.g., Florida Star, Inc. v. B.J.F., 491 U.S. 524 (1989) (holding that publication of truthful information lawfully obtained by newspaper was protected by First Amendment).

9. Cass R. Sunstein, "The President Who Would Bring Back the Sedition Act," https://www.bloomberg.com/opinion/articles/2018-08-29/trump-sees-sedition-in-google-s-algorithm (Aug. 29, 2018).

10. See Miami Herald Publ'g Co. v. Tornillo, 418 U.S. 241 (1974) (invalidating state right of reply law that required newspapers to publish replies of political candidates subject to critical coverage).

11. The story of the Zenger trial is told in Richard Kluger, *Indelible Ink: The Trials of John Peter Zenger and the Birth of America's Free Press* (W.W. Norton, 2016).

12. See Stephen D. Solomon, *Revolutionary Dissent: How the Founding Generation Created the Freedom of Speech* (St. Martin's Press, 2016).

13. See generally Geoffrey R. Stone, *Perilous Times: Free Speech in Wartime, From the Sedition Act of 1798 to the War on Terrorism* 5 (W.W. Norton, 2005). See also Thomas R. Reed, *America's Two Constitutions: A Study of the Treatment of Dissenters in Times of War* (Fairleigh Dickinson Univ. Press, 2017).

14. Stone, supra note 13, at 5.

15. Id. at 80–81.

16. Id. at 137.

17. Id. at 191.

18. Id. at 187.

19. Id. at 188.

20. Id. at 173.

21. The Court sustained convictions and lengthy prison terms in Abrams v. United States, 250 U.S. 616 (1919), Schenck v. United States, 249 U.S. 47 (1919), Frohwerk v. United States, 249 U.S. 204 (1919), and Debs v. United States, 249 U.S. 211 (1919).

22. *Abrams*, 250 U.S. at 629 (Holmes, J., dissenting).

23. Id. at 630.

24. Id. at 224.

25. See Gitlow v. New York, 268 U.S. 652 (1925); Whitney v. California, 274 U.S. 357 (1927).

26. *Gitlow*, 268 U.S. at 376.

27. Id.

28. Id. at 377.
29. 341 U.S. 494 (1951).
30. Stone, supra note 13, at 4.
31. Id. at 342 (calling the Committee "one of the great blunders" of the Truman presidency).
32. Id. at 348.
33. See, e.g., Watkins v. United States, 354 U.S. 178 (1957) (limiting congressional investigation powers). See also Arthur J. Sabin, *In Calmer Times: The Supreme Court and Red Monday* (Univ. of Penn. Press, 1999).
34. Yates v. United States, 354 U.S. 298 (1957).
35. See, e.g., Elfbrandt v. Russell, 384 U.S. 11 (1966).
36. 376 U.S. 254 (1964).
37. Id. at 279–80.
38. See id. at 273–76.
39. Id. at 276.
40. Letter to Mrs. Adams, July 22, 1804, 4 *Jefferson's Works* 555, 556 (Washington ed.).
41. *Sullivan*, 376 U.S. at 276.
42. Id. at 273.
43. Id. at 270.
44. Sweeney v. Patterson, 128 F.2d 457, 458 (1942).
45. *Sullivan*, 376 U.S. at 273.
46. Brandenburg v. Ohio, 395 U.S. 444, 445–46 (1969).
47. *Whitney*, 274 U.S. at 375 (Brandeis, J., concurring).
48. Id. at 376.
49. Id. at 375.
50. See Stone, supra note 13, at 487–90 (describing surveillance programs).
51. New York Times Co. v. United States, 403 U.S. 713 (1971).
52. Texas v. Johnson, 491 U.S. 397 (1989).
53. See, e.g., Laird v. Tatum, 408 U.S. 1 (1972); United States v. O'Brien, 391 U.S. 367 (1968).
54. *Abrams*, 250 U.S. at 630 (Holmes, J., dissenting).
55. Stone, supra note 13, at 557.

Chapter 3

1. West Va. State Bd. of Educ. v. Barnette, 319 U.S. 624 (1943).
2. For a discussion of the manner in which perceived and real foreign threats have influenced interpretation of the First Amendment, see Timothy Zick, *The Cosmopolitan First Amendment: Protecting Transborder Expressive and Religious Liberties* (Cambridge Univ. Press, 2013).
3. Here I will bracket whether the president's embrace of Christmas or Christianity might implicate the First Amendment's Establishment Clause, which prohibits government from adopting or endorsing particular faiths.

4. Vann R. Newkirk II, *No Country for Colin Kaepernick*, Atlantic (Aug. 11, 2017), https://perma.cc/T5GE-X5QP.

5. Eric Reid, "Why Colin Kaepernick and I Decided to Take a Knee," *N.Y. Times* (Sept. 25, 2017), https://www.nytimes.com/2017/09/25/opinion/colin-kaepernick-football-protests.html.

6. Jeremy Gottlieb & Mark Maske, "Roger Goodell Responds to Trump's Call to 'Fire' NFL Players Protesting during National Anthem," *Wash. Post* (Sept. 23, 2017), https://perma.cc/QUP4-ES7R.

7. See Samuel Perry & Andrew Whitehead, "What 'Make America Great Again' and 'Merry Christmas' Have in Common," *Huffington Post* (Dec. 20, 2018).

8. Kathryn Casteel, "How Do Americans Feel about the NFL Protests? It Depends on How You Ask," FiveThirtyEight (Oct. 9, 2017, 5:58 AM), https://perma.cc/TE5J-KYEK.

9. 319 U.S. 624 (1943).

10. Id. at 640.

11. Id. at 641.

12. Id.

13. West Va. State Bd. of Educ. v. Barnette, 319 U.S. 624 (1943).

14. Wooley v. Maynard, 430 U.S. 705 (1977).

15. Hurley v. Irish-American Gay, Lesbian and Bisexual Group of Boston, 515 U.S. 557 (1995).

16. See Janus v. AFSCME, 585 U.S. __, 138 S. Ct. 2448 (2018).

17. See National Institute of Family and Life Advocates v. Becerra, 585 U.S. ___, 138 S. Ct. 2361 (2018) .

18. Talley v. California, 362 U.S. 60 (1960).

19. E.g., Miami Herald Pub. Co. v. Tornillo, 418 U.S. 241 (1974).

20. 491 U.S. 397 (1989).

21. Id. at 414.

22. Id. at 417.

23. Id. See also Schacht v. United States, 398 U.S. 58 (1970) (invalidating federal law that permitted actors portraying service members to wear the uniform of an armed force "if the portrayal does not tend to discredit that armed force").

24. Johnson, 491 U.S. at 418.

25. Id. at 419.

26. Id. at 420.

27. Id. at 432 (Rehnquist, C.J., dissenting).

28. Public Support for Constitutional Amendment on Flag Burning (June 29, 2006), https://news.gallup.com/poll/23524/public-support-constitutional-amendment-flag-burning.aspx.

29. United States v. Eichman, 496 U.S. 310 (1990).

30. U.S. const., art. II, § 1, cl. 8.

31. U.S. const., art. IV, cl. 3.

32. See Harold Melvin Hyman, *To Try Men's Souls: Loyalty Tests in American History* (Praeger, 1982).

33. Baggett v. Bullit, 377 U.S. 360 (1964).

34. Elfbrandt v. Russell, 384 U.S. 11 (1966).

35. Keyishian v. Bd. of Regents, 385 U.S. 589 (1967).

36. Id. at 603.

37. *See* Robert Post, "Do Trump's NFL Attacks Violate the First Amendment?," Politico (Sept. 27, 2017), https://perma.cc/3WMV-522K.

38. See James E. Fleming & Linda C. McClain, *Ordered Liberty: Rights, Responsibilities, and Virtues* 4 (2013) (arguing that the state should use its persuasive powers to "help persons develop their moral capacities for self-government and, in that sense, live good lives"); Corey Brettschneider, *When the State Speaks, What Should It Say? How Democracies Can Protect Expression and Promote Equality* 73 (Princeton Univ. Press, 2012) (arguing that the state "should non-neutrally express and promote the values of free and equal citizenship").

39. See Whitney v. California, 274 U.S. 357, 375 (1927) (Brandeis, J., concurring) ("the fitting remedy for evil counsels is good ones").

40. John Stuart Mill, *On Liberty* (Longman, Roberts & Green, 1869).

Chapter 4

1. Harry Kalven Jr., "The Concept of the Public Forum," 1965 *Sup. Ct. Rev.* 1, 11–12.

2. NAACP v. Button, 371 U.S. 415, 433 (1963).

3. See generally Timothy Zick, *Speech Out of Doors: Preserving First Amendment Liberties in Public Places* (Cambridge Univ. Press, 2009).

4. Packingham v. North Carolina, 137 S. Ct. 1730, 1737 (2017).

5. David A. Graham, "The Shaky Basis for Trump's 'Law and Order' Campaign," *Atlantic* (July 12, 2016), https://perma.cc/DQ7N-NQ4H.

6. Nwanguma v. Trump, 903 F.3d 604 (6th Cir. 2018).

7. Brandenburg v. Ohio, 395 U.S. 444 (1969).

8. Maya Salam, "Case Is Dropped against Activist Who Laughed at Jeff Sessions's Hearing," *N.Y. Times* (Nov. 8, 2017), https://www.nytimes.com/2017/11/07/us/jeff-sessions-laughter-protester.html.

9. Unlike a public park, a congressional hearing room is not a "public forum" open to public expression. Still, prosecuting a non-disruptive chuckler suggests a lack of minimal tolerance for public disorder and dissent.

10. See Timothy Zick, "Protests in Peril," *U.S. News & World Rep.* (Nov. 20, 2017, 1:00 PM), https://www.usnews.com/opinion/civil-wars/articles/2017-11-20/prosecuting-inauguration-day-protesters-puts-free-speech-in-peril.

11. See Laurel Raymond, "Trump Still Silent Two Days after Protesters in DC Were Brutally Assaulted by Turkish Security," *ThinkProgress* (May 18, 2017, 3:59 PM), https://perma.cc/8Y5Y-PS34.

12. Khaled A. Beydoun & Justin Hansford, "The F.B.I.'s Dangerous Crackdown on 'Black Identity Extremists," *N.Y. Times* (Nov. 15, 2017), https://www.nytimes.com/2017/11/15/opinion/black-identity-extremism-fbi-trump.html.

13. Adam Goldman, "Trump Reverses Restrictions on Military Hardware for Police," *N.Y. Times* (Aug. 28, 2017), https://www.nytimes.com/2017/08/28/us/politics/trump-police-military-surplus-equip ment.html.

14. These examples are reported in Christopher Ingraham, "Republican Lawmakers Introduce Bills to Curb Protesting in at Least 18 States," *Wash. Post* (Feb. 24, 2017), https://perma.cc/HTG5-NRVW and Traci Yoder, "New Anti-protesting Legislation: A Deeper Look," *Nat'l Law. Guild* (Mar. 2, 2017), https://perma.cc/P5UT-6MMV.

15. See Alexander Sammon, "A History of Native Americans Protesting the Dakota Access Pipeline," *Mother Jones* (Sept. 9, 2016, 6:16 PM), https://perma.cc/RBU2-SESY (examining the events that led to the pipeline protests); Monica Davey & Julie Bosman, "Protests Flare after Ferguson Police Officer Is Not Indicted," *N.Y. Times* (Nov. 24, 2014), https://www.nytimes.com/2014/11/25/us/ferguson-darren-wilson-shooting-michael-brown-grand-jury.html (explaining events that led to the Ferguson protests); Gregory Krieg, "Police Injured, More than 200 Arrested at Trump Inauguration Protests in DC," CNN (Jan. 21, 2017, 4:06 AM), https://perma.cc/5AZ4-445S (examining events surrounding arrests of protesters at Trump inauguration).

16. *See* Harriet Agerholm, "More than 20 US States Have Cracked Down on Protests since Donald Trump's Election, *Independent* (May 9, 2017, 1:23 PM), https://perma.cc/MKU4-6RK8 (quoting UN report).

17. Packingham v. North Carolina, 137 S. Ct. 1730, 1737 (2017).

18. Gordon S. Wood, *The Creation of the American Public, 177–1787* 320 (UNC Press, 1969).

19. Id.

20. Stephen D. Solomon, *Revolutionary Dissent: How the Founding Generation Created the Freedom of Speech* 99–100 (St. Martin's Press, 2016).

21. Id. at 123–24.

22. John D. Inazu, *Liberty's Refuge: The Forgotten Freedom of Assembly* 34–35 (Yale Univ. Press, 2012).

23. Tabatha Abu El-Haj, "All Assemble: Order and Disorder in Law, Politics, and Culture," 16 *U. Pa. J. Const. L.* 949 (2014).

24. Id. at 969.

25. Id. at 969–70.

26. David Rabban, *Free Speech in Its Forgotten Years, 1870–1920* (Cambridge Univ. Press, 1997), ch. 2.

27. Davis v. Massachusetts, 167 U.S. 43 (1897).

28. 307 U.S. 496 (1939).

29. Id. at 515.

30. Zick, supra note 3, ch. 2.

31. For discussion of early cases involving restrictions on the expressive rights of Jehovah's Witnesses, see Stephen Feldman, "The Theory and Politics of First Amendment Protections: Why Does the Supreme Court Favor Free Expression over Religious Freedom?" 8 *U. Pa. J. Const. L.* 431, 443–51 (2006); David Hildebrand, "Free Speech and Constitutional Transformation," 10 *Const. Comment.* 133, 150–59 (1993).

32. Perry Educ. Ass'n v. Perry Local Educators' Ass'n, 460 U.S. 37, 45-46 (1983).

33. Kalven, supra note 1, at 11–12.

34. For an account of the NAACP's critical role in this process, see Harry Kalven Jr., *The Negro and the First Amendment* (Univ. Chicago Press, 1956).

35. Kalven, supra note 1, at 11–12.

36. Id. at 23.

37. Id.

38. Id. at 13.

39. Perry Educ. Ass'n v. Perry Local Educators' Ass'n, 460 U.S. 37, 45–46 (1983).

40. See Hudgens v. N.L.R.B., 424 U.S. 507 (1976) (holding that speakers have no First Amendment right to access private shopping malls).

41. Ward v. Rock Against Racism, 491 U.S. 781 (1989).

42. Kalven, supra note 1, at 12.

43. See Robert Post, *Constitutional Domains* 199 (Harvard Univ. Press, 1995) (contending that public forum doctrine is "virtually impermeable to common sense" and has received "nearly universal condemnation from commentators").

44. Whitney v. California, 274 U.S. 357, 372 (1927).

45. Zick, supra note 3, at 21 ("Speakers like abortion clinic sidewalk counselors, petition gatherers, solicitors, and beggars seek the critical expressive benefits of proximity and immediacy that inhere in such places.").

46. Timothy Zick, "Speech and Spatial Tactics," 84 *Texas L. Rev.* 581, 636 (2006).

47. Zick, supra note 3, ch. 4.

48. See generally Geoffrey R. Stone, "Content Neutrality and the First Amendment," 25 *Wm. & Mary L. Rev.* 189 (1983).

49. See Zick, supra note 3, at 25 ("The surface area of our expressive topography—the amount of public space that is available for and actually facilitates the exercise of First Amendment liberties—has been drastically shrinking for many decades.").

50. Id. at 36–43.

51. For discussions of protest policing methods, see Donnatella della Porta, H. Reiter & R. Reiner, *The Policing of Mass Demonstrations in Contemporary Democracies* (European University Institute, 1995); C. McPhail, D. Schweingruber & J. McCarthy, "Policing Protest in the United States: 1960-1995," in *Policing Protest: The Control of Mass Demonstrations in Western Democracies* (D. della Porta & H. Reiter eds., 1998); and L. Fernandez, *Policing Dissent: Social Control and the Anti-globalization Movement* (Rutgers U. Press, 2008).

52. J. McCarthy & C. McPhail, "The Institutionalization of Protest in the United States," in *The Social Movement Society* (D. Meyer & S. Tarrow eds.) (Rowman & Littlefield 1988).

53. Geoffrey R. Stone, *Perilous Times: Free Speech in Wartime, From the Sedition Act of 1798 to the War on Terrorism* 457–58 (W.W. Norton, 2005).

54. McCarthy & McPhail, supra note 52, at 96–100.

55. Id.

56. E. Maguire, "New Directions in Protest Policing," 35 *S.L.U. Pub. L. Rev.* 67, 83 (2015) (quoting A. Vitale, "The Command and Control and Miami Models at the

2004 Republican National Convention: New Forms of Policing Protests (2007) 12 *Mobilization* 403, 404, 406).

57. Stone, supra note 53, at 460.

58. *Packingham*, 137 S. Ct. at 1737.

59. Id. at 1735.

Chapter 5

1. Matal v. Tam, 137 S. Ct. 1744, 1764 (2017) (quoting United States v. Schwimmer, 279 U.S. 644, 655 (1929) (Holmes, J., dissenting)).

2. Karsten Muller & Carlo Schwarz, "Making America Hate Again? Twitter and Hate Crime under Trump," https://papers.ssrn.com/sol3/papers.cfm?abstract_ id=3149103 (Mar. 2018).

3. ADL, "2017 Audit of Anti-Semitic Incidents," https://www.adl.org/resources/ reports/2017-audit-of-anti-semitic-incidents#major-findings (Feb, 27, 2018).

4. See, e.g., Will Carless, "They Spewed Hate. Then They Punctuated It with the President's Name," https://www.pri.org/stories/2018-04-20/they-spewed-hate-then-they-punctuated-it-president-s-name (Apr. 20, 2018).

5. Executive Order on Improving Free Inquiry, Transparency, and Acccountability at Colleges and Universities, https://www.whitehouse.gov/presidential-actions/ executive-order-improving-free-inquiry-transparency-accountability-colleges-universities/ (Mar. 21, 2019).

6. Jeremy Waldron, *The Harm in Hate Speech* 8–9 (Harvard Univ. Press, 2012).

7. Brandenburg v. Ohio, 395 U.S. 444 (1969).

8. Chaplinsky v. New Hampshire, 315 U.S. 568 (1942).

9. Watts v. United States, 394 U.S. 705 (1969).

10. Virginia v. Black, 538 U.S. 343 (2003).

11. R.A.V. v. City of St. Paul, 505 U.S. 377 (1992).

12. The examples are taken from Waldron, supra note 6, at 8.

13. For a thorough discussion of these various harms, see generally id.

14. But see Nadine Strossen, *Hate: Why We Should Resist It with Free Speech, Not Censorship* 124–25 (Oxford Univ. Press, 2018) (expressing some doubts about the psychological harms typically said to be associated with "hate speech").

15. See Collin v. Smith, 578 F.2d 1197 (7th Cir. 1978). See also Phillipa Strum, *When the Nazis Came to Skokie: Freedom for the Thought We Hate* (Univ. of Kansas Press, 1999).

16. See Muller & Schwartz, supra note 2.

17. See, e.g., Cass R. Sunstein, *#Republic: Divided Democracy in the Age of Social Media* (Princeton Univ. Press, 2017).

18. Muller & Schwartz, supra note 2, at 3.

19. Waldron, supra note 6, at 65.

20. Id. at 96.

21. See, e.g., Toni M. Massaro, "Equality and Freedom of Expression: The Hate Speech Dilemma," 32 *Wm. & Mary L. Rev.* 211 (1991); Richard Delgado, "Words That

Wound. A Tort Action for Racial Insults, Epithets, and Name-Calling," 17 *Harv. C.R.-C.L. L. Rev.* 133 (1982).

22. See Mari Matsuda, "Public Response to Racist Speech: Considering the Victim's Story," 87 *Mich. L. Rev.* 2320, 2360 (1989).

23. See generally Keith E. Whittington, *Speak Freely: Why Universities Must Defend Free Speech* (Princeton Univ. Press, 2018); Erwin Chemerinsky & Howard Gillman, *Free Speech on Campus* (Yale Univ. Press, 2017). See also Robert Post, "The Classic First Amendment Tradition under Stress: Freedom of Speech and the University," https://papers.ssrn.com/sol3/papers.cfm?abstract_id=3044434 (Oct. 1, 2017).

24. See generally Strossen, supra note 14. Professor Strossen also discusses several important "procedural" objections to "hate speech" laws, including the inability to fashion a definition that is not unconstitutionally vague in the sense that its terms fail to place speakers on notice of their potential liability. That problem, and others, are in turn related to the lack of any accepted definition for "hate speech" as a category of communication.

25. Id. at 7.

26. R.A.V. v. City of St. Paul, 505 U.S. 377 (1992).

27. American Booksellers Ass'n v. Hudnut, 741 F.2d 323 (7th Cir. 1985), aff'd mem., 475 U.S. 1001 (1986).

28. See Charles R. Lawrence III, "If He Hollers Let Him Go, Regulating Racist Speech on Campus," 1990 *Duke L. J.* 430, 450–51.

29. 562 U.S. 443 (2011).

30. Id. at 460–61.

31. Abrams v. United States, 250 U.S. 616 (1919) (Holmes, J., dissenting).

32. Gertz v. Robert Welch, Inc., 418 U.S. 323 (1974).

33. Id.

34. Whitney v. California, 274 U.S. 357 (1927) (Brandeis, J., concurring).

35. See Strossen, supra note 14, at 7, chs. 4, 5, 7 (discussing research concerning enforcement of "hate speech" laws).

36. Id. at 15.

37. For this reason, among others, underrepresented minorities, who are disproportionately the target of hateful expression, do not uniformly agree that "hate speech" laws are the right approach to combatting racism.

38. Strossen, supra note 14, ch. 8.

39. Id. at 159–60.

40. Id. at 163–68.

41. Id. at 168–71.

42. *See* Pleasant Grove City v. Summum, 555 U.S. 640, 647 (2009) ("[I]f the government is engaging in [its] own expressive conduct, then the Free Speech Clause has no application.").

43. See generally James E. Fleming & Linda C. McClain, *Ordered Liberty: Rights, Responsibilities, and Virtues* (Harv. Univ. Press, 2013).

44. See *Summum*, 555 U.S. at 648 (noting that "government speech must comport with the Establishment Clause").

45. See Elizabeth S. Anderson & Richard H. Pildes, "Expressive Theories of Law: A General Restatement," 148 *U. Pa. L. Rev.* 1503, 1531–51 (2000) (focusing on equal protection and religious non-establishment limits on government speech).

46. See Trump v. Hawaii, 138 S. Ct. 2392, 2417–21 (2018) (reviewing evidence of "animus" in President Trump's statements, but holding that the statements did not invalidate the travel ban).

47. See U.S. const., amend. V, XIV. The Equal Protection Clause of the Fourteenth Amendment limits the actions and communications of states. As it has been interpreted, the Fifth Amendment's Due Process Clause contains an equal protection component. See Bolling v. Sharpe, 347 U.S. 497, 499 (1954).

48. Michael C. Dorf, "Same-Sex Marriage, Second-Class Citizenship, and Law's Social Meaning," 97 *Va. L. Rev.* 1267, 1275 (2011).

49. Id. at 1300.

50. See Nelson Tebbe, "Government Nonendorsement," 98 *Minn. L. Rev.* 648, 657–58 (2013) (positing a government "nonendorsement" principle based in equal protection, free speech, and due process principles).

51. See Dorf, supra note 48, at 1293–98 (discussing equality concerns relating to official enactments regarding sexual orientation). See also Helen Norton, "The Equal Protection Implications of Government's Hateful Speech," 54 *Wm. & Mary L. Rev.* 159 (2012) (addressing equal protection limits on government speech regarding homosexuality and gay rights); Deborah Hellman, "The Expressive Dimension of Equal Protection," 85 *Minn. L. Rev.* 1 (2000) (discussing equal protection concerns relating to laws regarding homosexuality).

52. See Tebbe, supra note 50, at 650 (arguing that government "nonendorsement" principle prohibits "any endorsement that abridges full and equal citizenship in a free society").

53. Id. at 666.

54. Id. at 667.

55. Id. at 667–68.

56. See Fleming & McClain, supra note 43, at 4 (arguing that the state should use its persuasive powers to "help persons develop their moral capacities for self-government and, in that sense, live good lives"); Corey Brettschneider, *When the State Speaks, What Should It Say? How Democracies Can Protect Expression and Promote Equality* (Princeton Univ. Press, 2012) (arguing that governments should engage in noncoercive persuasion to convince citizens to adopt liberal positions regarding gay equality and other rights); Abner S. Greene, "Government Endorsement: A Reply to Nelson Tebbe's Government Nonendorsement," 98 *Minn. L. Rev.* 87, 88 (2013) ("With a few limits, the state, as a representative of the people in their capacity as citizens, may and should take distinctive positions on contested issues to achieve certain public goods, and to teach what the state believes to be true.").

57. *See* Brettschneider, *supra* note 49, at 88–89 (discussing coercion and means-based limits on government persuasion).

58. Id. at 71–72.

59. Id. at 72.

60. Id.
61. Id. at 78.
62. Id. at 81.
63. Id. at 82.
64. Id. at 85.
65. See id. at 87 ("The challenge for value democracy, however, lies in simultaneously protecting rights of expression against coercive interference, while criticizing inegalitarian beliefs protected by these rights.").
66. Id. at 88.
67. Id. at 89.
68. See id. at 96 (urging that "more schools should teach and honor the contribution of Harvey Milk to equal rights for gays"); 131 (contenting that "the Boy Scouts of America should be denied the tax-exemption and tax-deductibility privileges of non-profit status").
69. Id. at 79 (observing that the state must "protect the free speech rights of citizens to make all arguments as speakers and to hear all arguments as listeners").
70. Trump v. Hawaii, 138 S. Ct. at 2417–28.

Chapter 6

1. Statement attributed to Edward R. Murrow.
2. Gregory P. Magarian, *Managed Speech: The Roberts Court's First Amendment* xi (Oxford Univ. Press, 2017).
3. Cass R. Sunstein, *Why Societies Need Dissent* 6–7 (Harvard Univ. Press, 2003).
4. Steven H. Shiffrin, *Dissent, Injustice, and the Meanings of America* xi (Princeton Univ. Press, 1999).
5. Id. at 77.
6. Id. at 42.
7. Lawrence B. Solum, "The Value of Dissent," 85 *Cornell L. Rev.* 859, 872 (2000).
8. Whitney v. California, 274 U.S. 357 (1927) (Brandeis, J., concurring).
9. Sunstein, supra note 3, at 110.
10. Id.
11. Id. at 97.
12. Shiffrin, supra note 4, at xii.
13. Id. at 104.
14. Stephen D. Solomon, *Revolutionary Dissent: How the Founding Generation Created the Freedom of Speech* 295–96 (St. Martin's Press, 2016).
15. Id. at 296.
16. Jack M. Rakove (ed.), *James Madison: Writings* 651 (Library of America, 1999).
17. Shiffrin, supra note 4, at xii.
18. See generally Timothy Zick, *Speech Out of Doors: Preserving First Amendment Liberties in Public Places* (Cambridge Univ. Press, 2009).
19. Sunstein, supra note 3, at 148.

20. Id. at 5–6; 25–26.

21. Id. at 11.

22. Id. at 112.

23. Id. at 138–40.

24. Steven H. Shiffrin, *The First Amendment, Democracy, and Romance* 91 (Harvard Univ. Press, 1990).

25. Sunstein, supra note 3, at 12.

26. Id. at 7.

27. John Stuart Mill, "On Liberty," in *On Liberty and Other Essays* 21 (John Gray ed., 1991).

28. See Tabatha Abu El-Haj, "All Assemble: Order and Disorder in Law, Politics, and Culture," 16 *U. Pa. J. Const. L.* 949 (2014).

29. See generally Geoffrey R. Stone, *Perilous Times: Free Speech in Wartime from the Sedition Act of 1870 to the War on Terrorism (W.W. Norton, 2005)* ; Thomas R. Reed, *America's Two Constitutions: A Study of the Treatment of Dissenters in Times of War* (Farleigh Dickinson Univ. Press, 2017).

30. 337 U.S. 1, 4 (1949).

31. Id.

32. 376 U.S. 254, 270 (1964).

33. See Schenck v. United States, 249 U.S. 47 (1919); Debs v. United States, 249 U.S. 211 (1919); Abrams v. United States, 250 U.S. 616 (1919).

34. Abrams v. United States, 250 U.S. 616, 629 (1919) (Holmes, J., dissenting); id. at 627.

35. Cantwell v. Connecticut, 310 U.S. 296, 308 (1940).

36. Id.

37. Id. at 310.

38. Id. at 309.

39. Chaplinsky v. New Hampshire, 315 U.S. 568, 573 (1942).

40. Id. at 569.

41. 340 U.S. 315 (1951).

42. Id. at 330 (Douglas, J., dissenting).

43. Id. at 317.

44. Id. at 330.

45. Id. at 320.

46. See Edwards v. South Carolina, 372 U.S. 229, 238 (1963) (invalidating breach of peace convictions of civil rights protesters); Cox v. Louisiana, 379 U.S. 536, 545 (1965) (invalidating convictions of civil rights demonstrators).

47. See Brown v. Louisiana, 383 U.S. 131, 143 (1966) (overturning convictions of group that refused to leave public library reading room when asked).

48. Tinker v. Des Moines Indep. Sch. Dist., 393 U.S. 503, 508 (1969).

49. See, e.g., Adderley v. Florida, 405 U.S. 39, 46 (1966) (upholding trespass convictions of civil rights protesters situated in curtilage of jailhouse).

50. See, e.g., Garner v. Louisiana, 368 U.S. 157, 163 (1961) (invalidating breach of peace convictions in sit-in case on procedural due process grounds).

51. See New York Times Co. v. Sullivan, 376 U.S. 254, 270 (1964) (invalidating state libel laws).

52. See Cohen v. California, 403 U.S. 15, 25 (1971).

53. 395 U.S. 444 (1969).

54. Id. at 445.

55. Id. at 446.

56. Terminiello v. City of Chicago, 337 U.S. 1, 4 (1949).

57. See United States v. O'Brien, 391 U.S. 367, 371 (1968) (upholding conviction for public burning of draft card); FCC v. Pacifica, 438 U.S. 726 (1978) (upholding order limiting time of day when indecent speech could be broadcast on the radio); Clark v. Cmty. for Creative Non-Violence, 468 U.S. 288 (1984) (upholding restrictions on overnight camping in national parks).

58. Perry Educ. Ass'n v. Perry Local Educators' Ass'n, 460 U.S. 37, 45–46 (1983).

59. Zick, supra note 18, at 25 ("The surface area of our expressive topography—the amount of public space that is available for and actually facilitates the exercise of First Amendment liberties—has been drastically shrinking for many decades.").

60. See Hudgens v. NLRB, 424 U.S. 507 (1976) (no First Amendment right to access private shopping malls).

61. See generally Zick, supra note 18.

62. Timothy Zick, "Speech and Spatial Tactics," 84 *Tex. L. Rev.* 581, 636 (2006).

63. See Robert Post, *Constitutional Domains* 199 (Harvard Univ. Press, 1995) (contending that the public forum doctrine is "virtually impermeable to common sense" and has received "nearly universal condemnation from commentators").

64. *See* Emily Ekins, "The State of Free Speech and Tolerance in America," *Cato Inst.* (Oct. 31, 2017), https://perma.cc/FK4D-PZCR (reporting findings of Recent Cato Institute survey of public attitudes concerning free speech).

65. Roper Center for Public Opinion Research, "Going Too Far: The American Public's Attitudes toward Protest Movements," *Cornell Univ.*, https://perma.cc/2A7M-759Z. (last visited Apr. 5, 2018).

66. Shiffrin, supra note 4, at 112-13.

67. See generally Lee C. Bollinger, *The Tolerant Society* (Oxford Univ. Press, 1988).

68. See generally Daniel Citron, *Hate Crimes in Cyberspace* (Harvard Univ. Press, 2014) (examining the trends of online harassment, stalking, and other actions that undermine the ability of women and minorities to participate in online discourse).

69. Stone, supra note 29, at 557.

Index

For the benefit of digital users, indexed terms that span two pages (e.g., 52–53) may, on occasion, appear on only one of those pages.